CHILDREN'S ISSUES, LAWS AND PROGRAMS

BARRIERS AND SUCCESS FACTORS IN ADOPTIONS FROM FOSTER CARE

CHILDREN'S ISSUES, LAWS AND PROGRAMS

Additional books in this series can be found on Nova's website under the Series tab.

Additional E-books in this series can be found on Nova's website under the E-books tab.

CHILDREN'S ISSUES, LAWS AND PROGRAMS

BARRIERS AND SUCCESS FACTORS IN ADOPTIONS FROM FOSTER CARE

BRADLEY J. CARSON
EDITOR

Nova Science Publishers, Inc.
New York

For permission to use material from this book please contact us:
Telephone 631-231-7269; Fax 631-231-8175
Web Site: http://www.novapublishers.com

NOTICE TO THE READER

LIBRARY OF CONGRESS CATALOGING-IN-PUBLICATION DATA

Barriers and success factors in adoptions from foster care / editor, Bradley
J. Carson.
p. cm.
Includes index.
ISBN 978-1-61209-740-4 (hardcover)
1. Adoption--United States--Statistics. 2. Foster home care--United
States--Statistics. 3. Special needs adoption--United States--Statistics.
I. Carson, Bradley J.
HV875.55.B357 2011
362.734--dc22
2011001115

Published by Nova Science Publishers, Inc. † New York

CONTENTS

PREFACE

This new book highlights a report to Congress which outlines the findings of two adoption-research studies conducted as part of The Collaboration to AdoptUsKids. In the first study, a nationwide purposive sample of 300 families seeking to adopt children with special needs from the public child welfare system was selected, interviewed and surveyed to determine actual and potential barriers to the completion of the adoption process. In the second study, a four-year prospective examination of a nationwide sample of 161 families who had adopted children with special needs was conducted in order to determine factors that contributed to successful adoption outcomes.

Chapter 1- This chapter to Congress outlines the findings of two adoption-research studies conducted as part of The Collaboration to AdoptUsKids. In the first study, a nationwide purposive sample of 300 families seeking to adopt children with special needs from the public child welfare system was selected, interviewed, and surveyed to determine actual and potential barriers to the completion of the adoption process. In addition, a nationwide sample of 382 private- and public- agency adoption staff members were surveyed to assess their opinions regarding barriers to the adoption process. This first study is referred to as the "Barriers" study in this chapter.

Chapter 2- : Adoption and Foster Care Analysis and Reporting System (AFCARS) FY 2009 data (October 1, 2008 through September 30, 2009).

Data from both the regular and revised AFCARS file submissions received by July 29, 2010 are included in the information below. Missing data are excluded from the distributions presented below.

Chapter 3- This chart includes data submitted to the Adoption and Foster Care Analysis and Reporting System (AFCARS) by States, the District of Columbia and Puerto Rico by July 29, 2010. Please note that, for all of the years shown, some of the data may differ from that shown in earlier versions of this chart. This is due to the fact that some States have resubmitted their AFCARS data after addressing data quality issues.

In: Barriers and Success Factors in Adoptions... ISBN: 978-1-61209-740-4
Editor: Bradley J. Carson

Chapter 1

BARRIERS & SUCCESS FACTORS IN ADOPTIONS FROM FOSTER CARE: PERSPECTIVES OF FAMILIES AND STAFF SUPPORTED BY THE ADOPTION OPPORTUNITIES PROGRAM

Children's Bureau, Administration on Children, Youth and Families

EXECUTIVE SUMMARY

This chapter to Congress outlines the findings of two adoption-research studies conducted as part of The Collaboration to AdoptUsKids. In the first study, a nationwide purposive sample of 300 families seeking to adopt children with special needs from the public child welfare system was selected, interviewed, and surveyed to determine actual and potential barriers to the completion of the adoption process. In addition, a nationwide sample of 382 private- and public- agency adoption staff members were surveyed to assess their opinions regarding barriers to the adoption process. This first study is referred to as the "Barriers" study in this chapter.

In the second study, a four-year prospective examination of a nationwide sample of 161 families who had adopted children with special needs was conducted in order to determine factors that contributed to successful adoption outcomes. This research study is referred to as the "Success Factors" study in this chapter. When all represented States are counted in both studies, family and staff participants came from all ten standard Federal regions, 47 States and the District of Columbia.

Below is a summary of demographics of participants and the major findings from each study.

BARRIERS STUDY

Barriers Study: Family Demographics

- Three hundred families who were in the process of adopting from the child welfare system were selected for participation in the Barriers study. Over the past four years, these families were interviewed periodically by telephone. At the close of data collection, July 1, 2007, 98 families (33 percent) had completed the process, received children and finalized their adoptions; 102 families (34 percent) had discontinued the process of adopting a child through the child welfare system; and 16 families (5 percent) were still continuing in the process. Among the 16 families who were still in the process of adopting, seven families (44 percent) had been approved to adopt but were waiting for children to be placed in their homes and nine families (56 percent) had children placed with them, but the adoptions had not yet been finalized. The remaining 84 families (28 percent) were re-contacted throughout the four-year period but for various reasons stopped responding to requests for updates, so their final adoption outcomes are unknown.
- In this chapter, data from the 102 families who discontinued the adoption process and the 98 families who finalized an adoption are highlighted (N = 200). These groups will be referred to as "discontinued" and "finalized."
- Of the 200 discontinued and finalized families, 183 (92 percent) were considered general adopter families (defined as families who did not have a prior relationship with the child they were adopting). Of these general adopters, 29 (16 percent) discontinued prior to completion of training and home study; 50 (27 percent) discontinued the adoption process after being approved; 17 (9 percent) discontinued the adoption

process after a disrupted placement; and 87 (48 percent) eventually finalized an adoption.

- Of the eight foster parent adopters, seven (88 percent) finalized an adoption and one (13 percent) discontinued after approval.[1] Among the seven child specific adopters, three (43 percent) finalized an adoption; two (29 percent) discontinued the adoption process after being approved; and two (28 percent) discontinued prior to completion of training and home study. Of the two relative adopters, one (50 percent) finalized an adoption, and one (50 percent) discontinued the adoption process prior to completion of training and home study.
- Among the 102 families who discontinued the adoption process, 59 (58 percent) were married couples, two (two percent) were unmarried same-sex couples, two (two percent) were unmarried opposite-sex couples, 29 (28 percent) were single females, and 10 (10 percent) were single males. The average age of this subsample of both prospective adoptive mothers and prospective adoptive fathers was 41. Prospective adoptive mothers averaged 17 years of education; prospective adoptive fathers averaged 15 years of education. Seventy-one (70 percent) of the discontinued families were Caucasian; 22 (22 percent) were African American; six (six percent) were interracial; two (two percent) were Hispanic; and one (one percent) classified themselves as "mixed" (i.e., both parents had the same ethnic/racial mix). The majority of discontinued families (n = 96, 94 percent) were general adopters, and of the discontinued families 88 (86 percent) reported that this was their first adoption.
- Of the 98 families who completed the process, received a child, and finalized their adoptions, the majority, (n = 60, 61 percent), were married couples; seven (seven percent) were unmarried same-sex couples; one (one percent) was an unmarried opposite-sex couple; 29 (30 percent) were single females; and one (one percent) was a single male. The average age of prospective adoptive mothers was 41, and the average age of prospective adoptive fathers was 42. Prospective adoptive mothers averaged 16 years of education, while prospective adoptive fathers averaged 14 years of education. Sixty- eight (69 percent) were Caucasian; 15 (15 percent) were African American; nine (nine percent) were interracial (i.e., race/ethnicity of parents is not identical); three (three percent) were Hispanic; two (two percent) classified themselves as "mixed;" and one (one percent) was Native

American. The majority of families (n = 87, 89 percent) who finalized their adoptions were general adopters.

- Over half (n = 81, 51 percent) of the 158 children adopted by these 98 families were female; 139 (88 percent) were part of a sibling group; 74 (47 percent) were over five years of age at time of placement; and 84 (53 percent) were racially mixed or children of color.

Adoption Barriers: Family Perspectives

- General adopter families who finalized an adoption as well as those who discontinued were similar in the types of children they wanted to adopt. Overall, families most desired to adopt females and children who were 11 or younger. Families indicated a willingness to adopt children of varying racial backgrounds; however, the majority of families desired to adopt Caucasian children. In both groups, many families were willing to consider adopting children who had experienced prenatal drug use, had learning disabilities, or ADD/ADHD, but were unwilling or unable to adopt children with multiple physical disabilities and children with HIV/AIDS.
- The motivations to adopt from foster care were similar among finalized and discontinued families. The most common reason among both groups was the desire to help a disadvantaged child, a child with special needs, or a child in foster care. Financial constraints was the second most common reason for adopting from foster care rather than adopting internationally or through a private agency.
- Parents who finalized their adoptions reported that, at the time of placement, the child issues they considered most challenging were medical needs (n = 34, 22 percent) and having a history of abuse and neglect prior to adoption (n = 34, 22 percent). Other challenging child issues that families mentioned were: ADHD (n = 29, 18 percent); educational needs (n = 26, 16 percent); behavioral problems (n = 22, 14 percent); and prenatal drug or alcohol exposure (n = 22, 14 percent).
- Parents of children whose adoptive placements disrupted (n = 19 children) reported that the most challenging child issues known at placement were ADHD, medical needs, behavioral problems, and educational needs.

- After in-depth analyses of the transcripts of interviews with the 200 (102 finalized and 98 discontinued) families, the participants were divided into the following five groups based on which steps in the adoption process they had completed: Group 1: Families who made an initial contact with an agency, may have attended orientation, and started or completed their initial application, but then discontinued the adoption process; Group 2: Families who had completed an application, but discontinued the adoption process prior to approval, during either the training or home study process; Group 3: Families who completed their home study and training, were approved, but never had a child placed with them; Group 4: Families with whom a child was placed, but the adoption disrupted prior to finalization and the family subsequently discontinued the adoption process; and Group 5: Families who completed the adoption process, received a child, and finalized the adoption.
- The families' experiences with the adoption process were coded to assess child, family, and agency barriers that each group of families encountered. Every barrier that families felt impacted their entire adoption process was identified, and these are discussed in this chapter as "overall barriers." After identifying the overall barriers, the list was narrowed to those "top barriers" that appeared to most negatively impact the families'adoption process.
- Families who finalized an adoption (Group 5) or discontinued after a disrupted placement (Group 4) were most likely to report agency barriers. Ninety-eight percent of the 98 families who had finalized adoptions and 82 percent of the 17 families with disrupted placements identified adoption process logistics as an agency barrier. In fact, adoption process logistics generally were reported as an "overall barrier" by increasingly more families as they moved further along in the adoption process: Group 1 = 60 percent; Group 2 = 81 percent; Group 3 = 94 percent; Group 4 = 82 percent; and Group 5 = 98 percent. When analyzing the prevalence of adoption process logistics as a "top barrier," a similar trend emerges: Group 1 = 20 percent; Group 2 = 41 percent; Group 3 = 51 percent; Group 4 = 41 percent; and Group 5 = 68 percent.
- Families who finalized an adoption (Group 5) were less likely to report family barriers than families in Groups 1 through 4 (all families who discontinued the process of adopting a child from foster care).

- Families in Group 4 (disrupted placement) experienced the highest frequency of child barriers (76 percent), but only 29 percent of the families in this group reported child factors to be among the top barriers that influenced their decision to discontinue the process of adopting a child from foster care.
- Families who discontinued the adoption process after approval or after a disrupted placement and families who finalized an adoption from foster care (Groups 3-5) reported the highest number of agency barriers overall. Families who finalized an adoption (Group 5) reported the highest number of agency barriers as top barriers in their adoption process.
- The number of child, family, and agency factors were all significantly related ($p < .05$) to the group assignment for families. Seventy-seven percent of families in Group 4 (disrupted placement) and 40 percent of families in Group 5 (finalized adoption) reported child factors to be overall barriers to their adoption process. All families in Group 1 (discontinued after orientation) and Group 4 (disrupted placement) reported family factors as barriers to their overall adoption process. Fifty percent of Group 5 families (finalized adoption) reported family factors. Families in all five groups reported agency factors as barriers to their overall adoption process: 80 percent of Group 1; 93 percent of Group 2; 100 percent of Group 3; 100 percent of Group 4; and 100 percent of Group 5.
- Family factor barriers were most frequently reported by Groups 1 and 4 with a mean of 2.0 and 2.6 factors, respectively. All other groups reported a mean of less than two family factors per family. Group 4 families (disrupted placement) reported a mean of 1.2 child factors. Groups 1, 2, 3 and 5 all reported a mean of less than one child factor.
- The most frequently reported agency factors were: agency emotional support, adoption process logistics, jurisdictional and inter-jurisdictional issues, and agency communication/responsiveness. All of these factors, except jurisdictional and inter-
- jurisdictional issues,[2] were significantly related ($p < .05$) to the family's stage of completion in the adoption process (Groups 1-5).

Barriers Study: Staff Demographics

- Approximately 1,659 surveys were sent to staff in 34 States and Washington, D.C. A total of 382 surveys (23 percent) were received from staff located in 29 States and the District of Columbia.[3]
- One hundred thirteen of the staff surveys (30 percent) were completed by staff working in private adoption agencies, and the majority (n = 269, 70 percent) were completed by staff working in public adoption agencies. Private-agency adoption workers typically contracted with the State (public) agency to place children from foster care into adoptive placements.

Adoption Barriers: Staff Perspectives

- Major agency barriers identified by staff in this study included the following: an inadequate pool of families; jurisdictional issues related to termination of parental rights (TPR); issues with the Interstate Compact on the Placement of Children (ICPC);[4] the size of worker caseloads; and the availability of post-adoption services (respite care, etc.).
- Major family barriers identified included: the type of child desired; criminal background of prospective parents; an inability to accept certain characteristics in a child's background; an unwillingness to access services or community resources; and the lack of experience with special needs children.
- Major child barriers identified included: older age of child (over 11); a history of, or engaging in, sexual perpetration; sexual acting-out behavior; the need for siblings (three or more) to be placed together; and behavior problems in the home.
- Additional analyses were conducted on responses from staff in the seven States with significant public and private agency representation to determine whether there were statistically significant differences between public and private agency staff members' perceptions of major agency, family, and child barriers.[5] Adoption agency staff from public agencies were significantly more likely ($p < .05$) than private agency staff to rate the following as major barriers to adoptive placements: a lack of families appropriate for adoption of children

with special needs (80 percent vs. 60 percent); issues with the Interstate Compact on the Placement of Children (ICPC) (64 percent vs. 34 percent); caseload size (63 percent vs. 42 percent); and prospective adoptive parents' inability or unwillingness to accept certain characteristics in a child's background or history (61 percent vs. 41 percent).

SUCCESS FACTORS STUDY

Success Factors Study: Family and Child Demographics

- There were 161 families, a total of 270 individual adoptive parents, who participated in the Success Factors study. These families had finalized their adoptions between one and 14 years earlier. Ninety-three families (58 percent) had worked with public agencies, and 68 (42 percent) had worked with private agencies. The majority of the families (n = 104, 65 percent) were married couples. There were also two (one percent) unmarried same- sex couples and three (two percent) unmarried opposite-sex couples. Forty-seven parents in the sample (29 percent) were single female adopters, and the five single males represented three percent of all adoptive parents. The majority of families (80 percent) identified their ethnic background as Caucasian (n = 128). Eighteen (11 percent) were African American, five (three percent) were Hispanic, and nine (six percent) families identified themselves as interracial couples. Overall, the majority of families (n = 105, 65 percent) adopted children of the same ethnic background as their own, while 56 families (35 percent) transracially adopted. Caucasian single women (58 percent) were significantly more likely than couples (30 percent) to have adopted at least one child of color.
- Of the 161 families, 106 (66 percent) had adopted more than one child, of whom 47 (44 percent) had adopted two children; 42 (40 percent) had adopted between three and five children; and 17 (16 percent) had adopted between six and 10 children. The majority of families (n = 94, 58 percent) were general adopters,[6] while the remaining families were either adopting a foster child already living in their home (n = 41, 25 percent), adopting a relative (n = six, four

percent), or adopting a specific child known to the family (n = 20, 12 percent).

- One child from each family selected into the sample was chosen as the focus of the research study. The "focus child" was selected based on the age of the child at placement, severity of the child's special needs, level of challenge the child presented to the parent(s), and length of time the child had been in the adoptive home. Of the 161 focus children, 89 (55 percent) were males, and 72 (45 percent) were females. Half of the 161 focus children (n = 80) were Caucasian (non-Hispanic), and the other half were children of color (n = 31 or 19 percent were African American, n = 20 or 12 percent were Hispanic, n = three or two percent were Native American, and n = 27 or 17 percent were mixed race/ethnicity).
- Focus children were an average of 6.5 years of age at placement into the adoptive home and had been in their adoptive homes an average of six years at the time of the interview. Seventy-four percent (n = 119) of focus children were between five and 17 at the time of placement. Of the 161 children, six (four percent) were between 13 and 17 when placed, and 39 (24 percent) were between nine and 12 at placement.

Successful Adoptions: Family Perspectives

- Parents most frequently characterized a successful special-needs adoption as having the following characteristics: 1) Parents were committed to the child and the child's adoption into the family; 2) The child was still living in the home and not behaving negatively; 3) The child was showing progress in the adoptive home; 4) The parent and child had bonded with each other; and 5) Parents were prepared to adopt a child with special needs and had realistic expectations of the child.
- Statistically significant differences were found in levels of support families received pre- and post-placement (p = .05). At the initial decision to adopt, 66 families (41 percent) had received positive reactions to their decision from both friends and family. By the time of post-placement, however, 119 families (74 percent) reported positive support of the adoption from both friends and families.
- Despite the "success of the adoptions," over half of all families (n = 93, 58 percent) described their child as difficult or very difficult to

parent. Children in the study exhibited an average of 10 difficult behaviors, including the following: violating rules of conduct (70 percent), verbal aggression (55 percent), physical aggression (48 percent), stealing (48 percent), and vandalism (31 percent).

- Over 75 percent of the families received an adoption subsidy or help with dental and routine medical care. The most commonly reported post-adoption services used were financial supports including adoption subsidies (89 percent), help with routine medical care (79 percent), and help with routine dental care (77 percent). Ninety percent or more of the families who received these three services found them very or extremely helpful.
- Sixty-three to 79 percent of families found various types of counseling, training, and support groups to be helpful. Between 69 percent and 76 percent of the families who were counseled on parenting skills, abuse, separation, sexual, and adoption issues found the counseling very or extremely helpful.
- Sixty-seven percent of the families found their child's individual therapy to be very or extremely helpful. At least two thirds of families found that 10 out of 11 types of counseling were very or extremely helpful, while 50 percent of families found counseling to prevent an out-of-home placement to be very or extremely helpful.
- Forty-one percent of families reported a problem with finding time to access services. Forty percent of families indicated a lack of confidence in services providers. Thirty-five percent reported that often insurance did not cover a needed service.
- Of the 161 families in the study, 27 families (17 percent) had no pre- or post-finalization contact with any birth or foster family members, and 48 families (30 percent) had contact with one or both of the child's birthparents either pre- or post-finalization. Of these 48 families, 19 (40 percent) had contact pre-finalization only, while 29 (60 percent) had contact post-finalization (including those who had contact both pre- and post- finalization). This chapter includes findings from an analysis of those 48 with birthparent contact and the 27 without contact with birth or foster family members.
- In general, families who had contact (either pre- or post-finalization) with the child's birthparents (n = 48) were more likely to have adopted a foster child already placed in their home or a child with whom they had a previous relationship (child-specific or relative adoption) than the 27 families who had no contact with the child's

birthparents or foster family members. Families who had pre-finalization only contact with one or both birthparents (n = 19) were more likely to have court-mandated visits with birthparents than parents who had contact post-finalization. Families who had pre-finalization only contact generally had more frequent contact than the families who had contact with the child's birthparents post-finalization. Families with pre-finalization only contact were more likely to have had supervised visits with the birthparents, whereas families who had post-finalization contact had a variety of types of contact, including cards, letters, and emails; phone calls; and supervised or unsupervised visits.

- When comparing families with no contact to those families who had some type of contact with birthparents, there were no statistically significant differences between minority/interracial adoptive families and Caucasian adoptive families. In addition, there were no statistically significant differences when comparing pre-finalization only contact with one or both birthparents and pre- and post-finalization or post-finalization only contact. Among Caucasian adoptive families, 35 percent had no contact and 65 percent had some type of contact. Of the 65 percent with some type of contact, 43 percent had pre-finalization only contact, and 57 percent had pre- and post-finalization or post- finalization only contact. Among minority/interracial adoptive families, 37 percent had no contact and 63 percent had some type of contact. Of the 63 percent with some type of contact, 33 percent had pre-finalization only contact and 67 percent had pre- and post- finalization or post-finalization only contact.
- There were statistically significant differences ($p < .05$) in the level of contact when examining the age at placement of the adopted child. For children whose families had no contact, the average age at placement was 4.69 years of age. For children whose families had some type of contact with birthparents, the average age at placement was 6.74 years.
- Families in this sample who adopted children who had experienced physical neglect were significantly more likely than families who adopted children who had not experienced physical neglect to have contact with one or both birthparents (76 percent v. 24 percent). This held true regardless of whether physical neglect was the sole cause of the child's removal from the birth family or occurred in combination

with other circumstances. There were no significant differences related to neglect, however, when comparing pre- finalization only contact and pre- and post-finalization or post-finalization only contact.

- There was a statistically significant relationship for families who were mandated to have contact pre-finalization and whether they had contact post-finalization ($p < .05$). For families who were mandated to have pre-finalization contact with one or both birthparents ($n = 20$), the majority did not continue the contact after finalization. Of those 20 families, 70 percent had pre-finalization only contact and 30 percent reported contact post-finalization. Of the 28 families[7] who were not mandated to have contact with birthparents pre-finalization, 82 percent had post-finalization contact with birthparents.
- Despite the parenting challenges, 141 parents (88 percent) believed their child's adoption was a success, 17 (11 percent) were not sure, and three (two percent) said their adoption was not a success. Attachment issues, significant behavioral problems of the child, and lack of services were cited as reasons that parents believed their adoptions were not successful.
- When asked to offer advice to prospective adoptive families, families in the study most frequently suggested that adoptive families should display commitment to the child and to the adoption process. They needed to be flexible, tolerant, and patient; love the child unconditionally; and maintain a sense of humor.
- When asked to offer advice to adoption agencies, adoptive families suggested that adequate resources and services, such as respite care, subsidies, support groups, and counseling, should be provided to *both* the family and the child.

I. Introduction

Since the mid 1980s, several Federal legislative initiatives have been instituted in order to increase opportunities for permanency for children in the public child welfare system. The number of adoptions of children from foster care has increased steadily in the years since the passage of the Adoption Assistance and Child Welfare Act of 1980 (AACWA), also known as the "Family Reunification Act." This legislation was passed in order to help facilitate the permanent placement of children, either through reunification with the birth family or, in cases where this was not possible, placement in an adoptive home. The Act established the principles of permanency planning for children in foster care by requiring the development of comprehensive case plans. In addition, AACWA placed limits on the amount of funding that States could receive for foster care services, thereby encouraging the establishment of services provided to children in their home rather than in foster care. AACWA also provided Federal funding to States to subsidize adoptions of special needs children. Yet, despite these measures, the legislation had little effect on slowing the entry of children into the foster care system.

In response to concerns regarding the growing number of children in foster care, Congress enacted the Adoption and Safe Families Act (ASFA) Public Law (P.L.) 105-89, in 1997. Hoping to facilitate quicker placement of children into permanent homes, Congress included more stringent timelines for parents with children in foster care by requiring States to pursue termination of parental rights (TPR) if a child has been in foster care for 15 out of the most recent 22 months. While the legislation stipulated that reasonable efforts should be made to reunify families when possible, the legislation encouraged States to plan concurrently for adoption while working toward the goal of family reunification, so that an adoptive placement could be made more quickly, should the State need to seek termination of parental rights. Other adoption-related provisions included the stipulation that States must implement policies and procedures for cross-jurisdictional placements and the establishment of a Federally funded adoption incentive program.

The Adoption Incentive Program provided incentives to States to increase the number of adoptions. Under the 2003 amendments to the program, incentive funds are awarded to States if they exceed the overall baselines for either foster child adoption, older child adoption, or special needs adoption. States receive $4,000 for each adoption over the established baseline with an additional $2,000 for each adoption that is finalized with a Title IV-E Adoption Assistance agreement (U.S. Department of Health and Human Services, 2006b). In 2005, 21 States qualified for incentive funds through the adoption incentive program, totaling over $11,568,000 (U.S. Department of Health and Human Services, 2006a).

In the years since ASFA was enacted, the number of adoptions has risen from approximately 31,000 in 1997 to over 51,000 in 2005 (U.S. Department of Health and Human Services, 2005). In 2002, a record number of foster children were adopted – approximately 53,000 (U.S. Department of Health and Human Services, 2006d). Currently, over three-fourths of all adoptions from the U.S. public child welfare system meet the criteria for "special needs adoptions" (U.S. General Accounting Office, 2002). The term "special needs adoptions" generally refers to adoption of children who are older, belong to a sibling group, or have physical, mental, or emotional problems. In addition, the term often refers to adoptions of children of color (Reilly & Platz, 2003).

Children adopted from the foster care system in 2005 were an average age of 6.7 years old at the time of adoption. An overwhelming majority of children were adopted by their foster parents (60 percent) or relatives (25 percent). Of the children adopted in 2005, 43 percent were Caucasian, 30 percent were African American, 18 percent were Hispanic, five percent were two or more races/ethnicities, two percent were an "unknown" race/ethnicity, one percent were Native American, and one percent were Asian (U.S. Department of Health and Human Services, 2006c).

Despite the dramatic increase in the number of children adopted from foster care, thousands of children are still awaiting adoption. According to the Adoption and Foster Care Analysis Reporting System (AFCARS), the data reporting system for children in foster care, of the 514,000 children in foster care in the in U.S. in 2005, 115,000 children (22 percent) were waiting to be adopted. Of these waiting children, only 66,000 (57 percent) have had their parental rights terminated. Over half of the children waiting to be adopted are children of color. Children waiting to be adopted were an average of five years old when removed from their birthparents and by September 2005 were an average age of 8.6 years old (U.S. Department of Health and Human Services, 2007).

A. Background of Research

Several Federal initiatives in recent years have called for research in order to better understand the process of adopting and increase the success of adoptions from foster care. Ongoing concerns regarding the need to find adoptive homes for waiting children in the U.S. led to a legislative requirement to provide a report to Congress on the "Dynamics of Successful Adoption." Found in Section 204 of the Keeping Children and Families Safe Act of 2003 (P. L. 108-36), the research requirement was described as follows:

> *The Secretary shall conduct research (directly or by grant to, or contract with, public or private nonprofit research agencies or organizations) about adoption outcomes and the factors affecting those outcomes. The Secretary shall submit a report containing the results of such research to the*

appropriate committees of the Congress not later than the date that is 36 months after the date of the enactment of the Keeping Children and Families Safe Act of 2003.

Similarly, Section 330G(c) of the Public Health Service Act required the following research studies:

With respect to the adoption of children with special needs, the Secretary shall make grants to carry out studies to identify (A) the barriers to completion of the adoption process; and (B) those components that lead to favorable long-term outcomes for families that adopt children with special needs.

Although a report to Congress is not required, findings from this research are provided as an informational resource.

In 2002, the Adoption Exchange Association was awarded a five-year contract from the U.S. Children's Bureau to establish The Collaboration to AdoptUsKids in order to design and implement a national adoptive family recruitment and retention strategy aimed to increase the number of adoptions from foster care. As part of The Collaboration and in order to comply with the preceding legislative requirements, the University of Texas at Austin School of Social Work was awarded a contract to conduct the two Congressionally mandated studies.

In keeping with the Congressional requirements, over the past four years, two research studies have been conducted to assess barriers and success factors in special needs adoptions. Families and staff were recruited for participation in both the Barriers study (Study 1) and the Success Factors study (Study 2) primarily through direct contact with public and private adoption-agency staff and members of The Collaboration to AdoptUsKids (The Adoption Exchange Association, The Child Welfare League of America, The Northwest Adoption Exchange, The Adoption Exchange Education Center, and Holt International Children's Services). Specific criteria for the types of families needed was given to The Collaboration to AdoptUsKids workgroup members in an effort to help in the recruitment of families for inclusion in both the Barriers study and the Success Factors study. Special attention was placed on including families in the Barriers study who: were first time adopters; were early in the application process; were not trying to adopt a foster child who was in their home; and who did not have a child placed in their home for adoption.

In the Barriers study, a nationwide purposive sample of 300 families seeking to adopt children with special needs from the public child welfare system was selected from public and private agencies in 44 States and the District of Columbia. The families were followed from initial inquiry through finalization of their child's adoption. Interview and survey data were collected and analyzed in order to assess reasons why families chose to follow through with an adoption or discontinue the process. Three hundred eighty-two private and public agency staff from 29 States and the District of Columbia were surveyed to assess their opinions regarding barriers and to elicit suggestions for addressing barriers.

In the Success Factors study, a four-year prospective examination was conducted of a nationwide sample of 161 families from 34 States and the District of Columbia who had adopted children with special needs. Special attention was placed on including families who had adopted older children (particularly between the ages of 12-16 years), sibling groups, and children who had been in the foster care system for several years, in order to glean information on how these families and children were adjusting and what factors contributed to positive outcomes. Adoptive parents were interviewed by research staff and periodically administered surveys, including the Parenting Stress Inventory (Abidin, 1995) and a marital satisfaction scale. The following report presents the findings from both of these studies.

B. Protection of Human Subjects

Prior to the initiation of family recruitment, the Principal Investigator and project staff developed the protocol for the research studies and family and staff data collection instruments. The protocol and instruments were submitted for approval to The University of Texas at Austin Institutional Review Board (UT-IRB). The IRB committee granted approval before data collection began. Continuing Review applications were submitted every year for re-approval of both studies. In addition, several of the participating public agencies reviewed and approved the UT-IRB process and/or required a separate application and approval from their agency before participation.

II. Study 1

Barriers Study: Methods and Demographics

A. Methods

The goal of the Barriers study was to identify actual and potential barriers to the completion of the adoption process from the perspective of a nationwide sample of 300 families seeking to adopt children from the foster care system. These families were seeking to adopt from public and private agencies. It is important to note that the private agencies contracted with the State (public) agencies to facilitate adoptions of children from foster care. As families entered the study, they were assigned to one of two categories: 1) "Continuing" if they were in the process of adopting a child from the foster care system or 2) "Discontinued" if they had ceased the process of adopting a child from the foster care system. Continuing families may have been at any point in the process, from the initial adoption application to a completed home study and awaiting placement. Some of these families may have applied originally through one agency and then worked with another agency, but were still continuing the process. The majority of prospective adopters were experiencing the process for the first time and had not yet had a child placed in their home when they began participation in the study. There were, however, a few families included in the sample who had adopted previously (and were participating in this study while they were seeking to adopt for the second or third time) or already had received a child, but the adoption was not finalized. "Discontinued" families were either no longer seeking to adopt at all or were no longer seeking to adopt a child from the foster care system. The latter group of families decided to pursue international adoption or the adoption of an infant through a private agency.

1. Initial Data Collection

Initially, adoption agencies mailed "family packets" to prospective adoptive families qualifying for participation in the study. Families interested in participating were asked to return their packets to the University of Texas Research Team. These packets included consent forms for participation and a demographic form to be completed by families. Participating families then completed an "Adoption Process Questionnaire," which consisted of a series of 21 questions to assess which parts of the adoption process had been completed at the point of enrollment in the study. Upon completion of the process questionnaire, research team members used a structured interview schedule to conduct telephone interviews (usually between one and one half hours) to gather detailed information about the parts of the adoption process completed by the participant at the time of the interview. Discontinued families were given the option of completing an interview or a mailed survey and were asked questions about all parts of the process that they had completed prior to discontinuing their efforts to adopt from foster care. All interviews were transcribed verbatim.

2. Follow-up Data Collection

Upon completion of the initial interview, continuing prospective adoptive families were sent a follow-up survey every four months until a child was placed in the home and the adoption was finalized, or until the family decided to discontinue trying to adopt a child from the foster care system. This survey included questions about their experiences attempting to adopt since the initial data collection period.

3. Exit Interviews

Families exited the study in one of three ways: 1) through finalizing the adoption of a child placed in their home; 2) by choosing to discontinue the adoption process of a child from foster care (which moved the family into the discontinued category); or 3) by choosing to withdraw from the study. Exit telephone interviews were conducted with families falling into the first two groups. These interviews contained questions pertaining to their experiences since the last interview and finalization of the adoption, or where appropriate, questions pertaining to the reasons for discontinuing their plan to adopt from foster care. An illustration of the process of data collection in this prospective study is provided below:

4. Coding Methodology

Codebooks were developed and tested. Transcribed interviews were then coded by the Barriers study coding team, which was comprised of 13 staff members: two experienced coders (doctoral students) who served as team leaders and 11 graduate students trained by the team leaders. Coder training entailed two three-hour classes for each of the three codebooks used, followed by the whole team coding and consensing together one to three cases until the team demonstrated acceptable reliability. After training, adoptive family interviews were assigned to a pair of trained coders. After independent coding by the two team members, the pair met for consensus to resolve any areas of disagreement by choosing the most appropriate code. The codes were then checked by one of the two coding team leaders to ensure group reliability as a whole. Individual coding team members were randomly rotated to ensure that the various pairs of coders were following the same decision-making conventions. The two coding team leaders also coded cases, rotating through working with different team members.

B. Demographic Characteristics of Family Participants

1. Family Structure: Initial Data Collection

A sample of 300 families was selected to participate in the Barriers study. The majority, 62 percent, were married couples, four percent were unmarried same-sex couples, one percent were unmarried opposite-sex couples, 28 percent were single females, and five percent were single males.

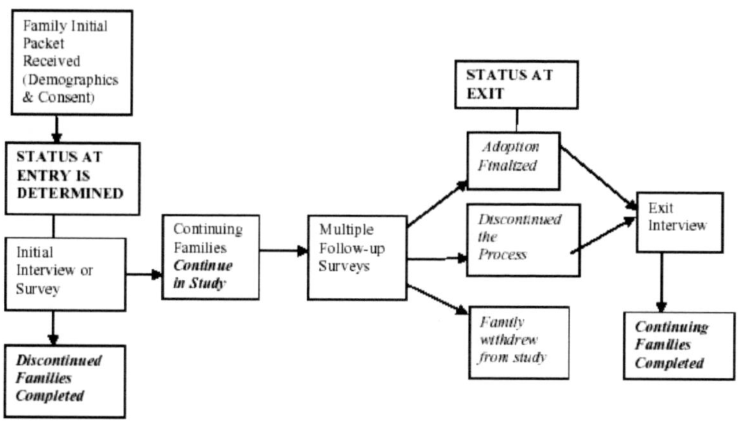

Figure 1. Barriers Study Data Flow

Table 1. Family Structure

Family Structure	Number	Percent
Married couples	185	62%
Unmarried couples-same sex	11	4%
Unmarried couples-opposite sex	3	1%
Single females	85	28%
Single males	16	5%
Total	**300**	**100%**

2. *Family Status*

At the time of initial data collection, 252 (84 percent) families were continuing the process of adopting and 48 (16 percent) families had discontinued the process.

3. *Age, Education, and Family Income*

The average age of the prospective adoptive mothers participating in the Barriers study was 41 years and prospective fathers was 43 years. Prospective adoptive mothers had completed an average of 16 years of education and fathers an average of 15 years of education. There were no significant differences in the income level of those who were continuing the adoption process and those who chose to discontinue. The families who were continuing in the adoption process had an average income of $72,399; the families who had discontinued had $71,956.

4. *Family Race/Ethnicity by Family Status*

Participants were each asked to identify their ethnic background. In cases in which each parent was racially/ethnically mixed, the couple was considered of “mixed race/ethnicity” (e.g., male is Caucasian and African American as well as the female is Caucasian and African American). Interracial couples were those in which the participants were of different ethnicities. In this sample, there were 23 interracial couples (n = 23; 18 continuing; 5 discontinued). Most prospective adoptive families in the study were Caucasian (n = 195; 163 continuing; 32 discontinued). The second largest group in the study was African American families (n = 59, 48 continuing, 11 discontinued). There were no Native American, Asian, Hispanic, or mixed race/ethnicity families in the sub-sample of families who had already discontinued at study entry.

5. *Family Race/Ethnicity by Type of Agency*

Family race/ethnicity is presented in Table 3 according to type of agency used. Almost all families were more likely to use private than public agencies but African American, Hispanic, and interracial families were twice as likely to use private agencies than public agencies: African American (n = 42 private; n = 17 public); Hispanic families (n = 10 private; n = five public); and interracial families (n = 16 private; n = seven public). Of the three Native American families, one used a private agency and two used a public agency.

Table 2. Family Race/Ethnicity by Family Status*

Status	Native American	Asian	African American	Hispanic	Inter-racial	Mixed Race/ Ethnicity	Caucasian (non-Hispanic)	Total Families
Continuing	3 (1%)	1 (1%)	48 (19%)	15 (6%)	18 (7%)	4 (2%)	163 (65%)	252 (84%)
Discontinued	0 (0%)	0 (0%)	11 (23%)	0 (0%)	5 (10%)	0 (0%)	32 (67%)	48 (16%)
Total**	**3 (1%)**	**1 (< 1%)**	**59 (20%)**	**15 (5%)**	**23 (8%)**	**4 (1%)**	**195 (65%)**	**300 (100%)**

*Percentages are calculated on the total for each row (e.g., n = 252 for continuing families).

**Percentages do not always add to 100% due to rounding.

Table 3. Family Race/Ethnicity by Type of Agency*

Status	Native American	Asian	African American	Hispanic	Inter-racial	Mixed Race/ Ethnicity	Caucasian (non-Hispanic)	Total Families
Private	1 (33%)	1 (100%)	42 (71%)	10 (67%)	16 (70%)	2 (50%)	103 (53%)	175 (58%)
Public	2 (67%)	0 (0%)	17 (29%)	5 (33%)	7 (30%)	2 (50%)	92 (47%)	125 (42%)
Total**	**3**	**1**	**59**	**15**	**23**	**4**	**195**	**300 (100%)**

*Percentages are calculated on the total for each column (e.g., n = 3 for Native American).

**Percentages do not always add to 100% due to rounding.

6. Adoptive Parent Sample

Three hundred families who were in the process of adopting from the child welfare system were selected for participation in the Barriers study. Over the four years of the study, these families were interviewed periodically by telephone. At the close of data collection on July 1, 2007, 98 families (33 percent) had completed the process, received children, and finalized their adoptions; 102 families (34 percent) had discontinued the process of adopting a child through the child welfare system; and 16 families (five percent) were still continuing in the process. Among thc 16 families who were still in the process of adopting, seven families had been approved to adopt but were waiting for children to be placed in their homes and nine families had children placed with them, but the adoptions had not yet been finalized. The remaining 84 families (28 percent) were re-contacted throughout the four-year period but for various reasons stopped responding to requests for updates, so their final adoption outcome is unknown. In this chapter, data from the 102 families who discontinued the adoption process and the 98 families who finalized an adoption are highlighted (N = 200). These groups will be referred to as "discontinued" and "finalized."

III. STUDY 1

Barriers Study: Family Perspectives

A. Sample Description

1. Type of Adoption by Family Status

The results presented in this section are based on data collected from 200 families (98 who finalized an adoption and 102 who discontinued the adoption process). As shown in Table 4, the majority of the 200 families (n = 183, 92 percent) in the Barriers study were general adopters (families who adopted a child with whom they had no prior relationship) (96 discontinued; 87 finalized adoptions). Of the remaining 17 families, eight were seeking to adopt a foster child in their home (one discontinued; seven finalized adoptions); two were applying to adopt a relative (one discontinued; one finalized adoption); and seven families were applying to adopt a specific child (non-relative) with whom they were acquainted, but had not fostered (four discontinued; three finalized adoptions). Typically, families who were trying to adopt specific children with whom they were already acquainted had met these children in a variety of ways: as their therapist, teacher, residential treatment worker, and/or through family or friends who were fostering the children. After meeting and interacting with the children, the families decided they wanted to adopt them and began the adoption process.

2. Point of Completion by Type of Adoption

As noted in Table 5, 87 of the 183 general adopters (48 percent) eventually finalized an adoption, 17 (nine percent) discontinued the adoption process after a disrupted placement, 50 (27 percent) discontinued the adoption process after being approved for adoption, and 29 (16 percent) discontinued prior to the completion of training and a home study. Of the eight foster parent adopters, seven (88 percent) finalized an adoption and one (13 percent) discontinued after approval.[8] Of the seven child specific adopters, three (43 percent) finalized an adoption, two (29 percent) discontinued the adoption process after being approved, and two (29 percent) discontinued prior to the completion of training and a home study. Of the two relative adopters, one (50 percent) finalized an adoption and one (50 percent) discontinued the adoption process prior to the completion of training and a home study.

3. Type of Child Family Desired to Adopt

This section provides data related to the first research question: what kind of children families most desired to adopt.

The sample of 183 general adopters were asked about the types of children they most desired to adopt, were willing to adopt, and were unwilling or unable to adopt. Overall, families most desired to adopt females and children aged 11 or younger. Families indicated a willingness to adopt children of varying racial backgrounds; however, the majority of families desired to adopt Caucasian children. Many families said they were willing to consider adopting children who experienced prenatal drug use, had learning disabilities, or had ADD/ADHD, but were unwilling or unable to adopt children with multiple handicaps or children with HIV/AIDS. Very few families indicated they most desired children with the following special needs: HIV/AIDS, prenatal drug exposure, physical disabilities, medical fragility, those with a prior history of sexual abuse or sexual acting out, multiple handicaps, learning disabilities, or ADD/ADHD.

Table 4. Type of Adoption by Family Status*

Status	General Adopters	Adopting Foster Child in the Home	Adopting a Relative	Applying to Adopt Specific Child NOT in the Home	Total Families
Discontinued	96 (94%)	1 (1%)	1 (1%)	4 (4%)	102 (100%)
Finalized	87 (89%)	7 (7%)	1 1%)	3 (3%)	98 (100%)
Total**	**183 (92%)**	**8 (4%)**	**2 (1%)**	**7 (4%)**	**200 (100%)**

*Percentages are calculated on the total for each row (e.g., n = 102 for discontinued families).

**Percentages do not always add to 100% due to rounding.

During the interviews, families frequently made comments expressing their discomfort with having to indicate to agencies what type of child they desired to adopt and what type of child they were unwilling or unable to adopt. Families who were required by agencies to complete "type of child" forms for their adoption application expressed similar discomfort with this request.[9]

Table 5. Point of Completion by Type of Adoption*

Total**	**5 (3%)**	**27 (14%)**	**53 (27%)**	**17 (9%)**	**98 (49%)**	**200 (100%)**
	Application	**raining/Home study**	**(No Placement)**	**(No Finalization)**		
General adoption	4 (2%)	25 (14%)	50 (27%)	17 (9%)	87 (48%)	183 (100%)
Foster adoption	0 (0%)	0 (0%)	1 (13%)	0 (0%)	7 (88%)	8 (100%)
Child specific adoption (non-relative)	1 (14%)	1 (14%)	2 (29%)	0 (0%)	3 (43%)	7 (100%)
Relative/ kin adoption	0 (0%)	1 (50%)	0 (0%)	0 (0%)	1 (50%)	2 (100%)

*Percentages are calculated on the total for each row (e.g., n = 183 for general adoption).

**Percentages do not always add to 100% due to rounding.

Table 6. Gender Desired by Family*

Gender	**Male**	**Female**
Most desired	73 (40%)	97 (53%)
Willing to adopt	89 (49%)	75 (41%)
Unwilling/unable	21 (11%)	11 (6%)
Total**	**183**	**183**

*Percentages are calculated on the total number of general adopter families in the sample (n = 183 families).

**Percentages do not always add to 100% due to rounding.

Table 7. Age of Child Desired by Family*

Age	< 1 mo	1 mo - 11 mo	1 - 2 yrs	3 - 4 yrs	5 - 11 yrs	12 - 18 yrs
Most desired	59 (32%)	59 (32%)	77 (42%)	69 (3 8%)	46 (25%)	16 (9%)
Willing to adopt	56 (3 1%)	56 (3 1%)	64 (35%)	78 (43%)	91 (50%)	38 (21%)
Unwilling/ unable	68 (37%)	68 (37%)	42 (23%)	36 (20%)**	46 25%)	129 (70%)
Total**	**183**	**183**	**183**	**183**	**183**	**183**

*Percentages are calculated on the total number of general adopter families in the sample (n = 183 families).

**Percentages do not always add to 100% due to rounding.

Table 8. Race/Ethnicity of Child Desired by Family*

Race/ Ethnicity	Caucasian	African Am.	Hispanic	Native Am.	Asian	Mixed Race/Ethnicity
Most desired	82 (45%)	50 (27%)	45 (25%)	34 (19%)	30 (16%)	49 (27%)
Willing to adopt	75 (4 1%)	88 (48%)	119 (65%)	113 (62%)	118 (64%)	122 (67%)
Unwilling/unable	26 (14%)	45 (25%)	19 (10%)	36 (20%)	35 (19%)	12 (7%)
Total**	**183**	**183**	**183**	**183**	**183**	**183**

*Percentages are calculated on the total number of general adopter families in the sample (n = 183 families).

**Percentages do not always add to 100% due to rounding.

4. Adoption Exchange Registration

This section provides data related to the second research question: what percentage of the families were registered on AdoptUsKids or another adoption exchange.

In the Barriers study, 98 families who had finalized their adoptions were asked if they had registered with an adoption exchange, and if so, which and how many exchanges. As noted in Table 10, a total of 58 families (59 percent) indicated that they registered on at least one exchange. The most common response was registration on State-specific exchanges (n = 36, 37 percent) and the second most common registration was on AdoptUsKids (n = 33, 34 percent).

Table 9. Special Needs of Child Desired by Family*

Special Needs	Inter-Country[10]	HIV/AIDS	Prenatal Drug Exp.	Siblings	Sexually Abused
Most desired	17 (9%)	2 (1%)	4 (2%)	60 (33%)	3 (2%)
Willing to adopt	12 (70%)	49 (27%)	137 (75%)	93 (51%)	136 (74%)
Unwilling/unable	38 (21%)	132 (72%)	42 (23%)	30 (16%)	44 (24%)
Total**	**18**	**183**	**183**	**183**	**183**

Special Needs	Medically Fragile	Phys. Disability	Sexual Acting Out	Multiple Handi-caps	Learning Disability	ADD/ ADHD
Most desired	4 (2%)	5 (3%)	2 (1%)	2 (1%)	10 (5%)	9 (5%)
Willing to adopt	87 (48%)	97 (53%)	74 (40%)	48 (26%)	157 (86%)	150 (82%)
Unwilling/ unable	92 (50%)	81 (44%)	107 (58%)	133 (73%)	16 (9%)	24 (13%)
Total**	**183**	**183**	**183**	**183**	**183**	**183**

*Percentages are calculated on the total number of general adopter families in the sample (n = 183 families).

**Percentages do not always add to 100% due to rounding.

Table 10. Adoption Exchange Registration*

Type of Adoption Exchange	Families Registered	%
State-Specific	36	37%
AdoptUsKids	33	34%
Local	7	7%
Agency-Specific	6	6%
Multi-State	6	6%
Other	4	4%
Did not specify	0	0%
Total registered on at least one exchange**	**58**	**59%**

*Percentages are calculated on the total number of families registered on an exchange (n = 98 families).

**Some families were registered on more than one exchange and therefore the percentages and n's do not add up to the total number of respondents (n = 98), or 100%.

5. Characteristics of Discontinued Families

a. Age, Education, and Family Income

This section provides data related to the third research question in this study: what are the characteristics of families who ***discontinued*** the process.

Of the 102 families in the Barriers study who discontinued the adoption process, the average age of both prospective adoptive mothers and prospective adoptive fathers was 41. Prospective adoptive mothers averaged 17 years of education; prospective adoptive fathers averaged 15 years of education. The average family income of families who discontinued the adoption process was $73,242. The average family income for couples was $87,219; $47,969 for single females; and $62,389 for single males.

b. Family Race/Ethnicity

Participants were asked to identify their ethnic background. In cases in which each parent was racially/ethnically mixed, the couple was considered of "mixed race/ethnicity" (e.g., Caucasian and African American male and Caucasian and African American female). Interracial couples are those in which the participants were of different ethnicities. Of the 102 discontinued families, 71 families (70 percent) identified themselves as Caucasian (non-Hispanic), 22 families (22 percent) identified themselves as African American, six families (six percent) were interracial, two families (two percent) identified themselves as Hispanic, and one family (one percent) was of mixed race/ethnicity.

Table 11. Family Race/Ethnicity*

Race/Ethnicity	Number	Percent
Caucasian (non-Hispanic)	71	70%
African American	22	22%
Interracial	6	6%
Hispanic	2	2%
Mixed race/ethnicity	1	1%
Asian	0	0%
Native American	0	0%
Total**	**102**	

*Percentages are calculated on the total number of discontinued families (n = 102).
**Percentages do not always add to 100% due to rounding.

Table 12. Family Structure*

Family Type	Number	Percent
Married couples	59	58%
Unmarried couples-same sex	2	2%
Unmarried couples-opposite sex	2	2%
Single females	29	28%
Single males	10	10%
Total	**102**	**100%**

*Percentages are calculated on the total number of discontinued families (n = 102).

Table 13. Type of Adoption*

Type of Adoption	Number	Percent
General adoption	96	94%
Child specific adoption (non- Relative)	4	4%
Foster adoption	1	1%
Relative/Kin adoption	1	1%
Total	**102**	**100%**

*Percentages are calculated on the total number of discontinued families (n = 102).

c. Family Structure

Of the 102 families in the sample who discontinued the adoption process, 59 (58 percent) were married couples, one (one percent) were unmarried same-sex couples, two (two percent) were unmarried opposite-sex couples, 29 (28 percent) were single females, and 10 (10 percent) were single males.

d. Type of Adoption

Of the 102 discontinued families in the Barriers study, the majority (n = 96, 94 percent) were considered general adopters. Four families (four percent) applied to adopt a specific child, one family (one percent) desired to adopt a child they were fostering, and one family (one percent) applied to adopt a relative.

e. Prior Adoption Experience

Out of 102 discontinued families, the majority of families (n = 88, 86 percent) were applying to adopt for the first time. However, nine families (nine percent) were adopting for the second time and four families (four percent) for the third or fourth time.

6. Characteristics of Finalized Families

This section provides data related to this study's fourth research question: what are the characteristics of families who successfully completed the adoption process by ***finalizing*** an adoption.

a. Age, Education, and Family Income

Of the 98 families who completed the process and finalized their adoptions, the average age of prospective adoptive mothers was 41, and the average age of prospective adoptive fathers was 42. Prospective adoptive mothers averaged 16 years of education; prospective adoptive fathers averaged 14 years of education. The average family income of families who finalized the adoption process was $73,114. Average income for couples was $85,005; $42,424 for single females; and $35,000 for single males.

b. Family Race/Ethnicity

Of the 98 finalized families, 68 families (69 percent) identified themselves as Caucasian (non-Hispanic), 15 families (15 percent) identified themselves as African American, nine families (nine percent) were interracial, three families (three percent) were Hispanic, two families (two percent) were mixed, and one family (one percent) was Native American.

c. Family Structure

Of the 98 families in the sample who finalized an adoption, 60 (61 percent) were married couples, seven (seven percent) were unmarried same-sex couples, one (one percent) was an unmarried opposite-sex couple, 29 (30 percent) were single females, and one (one percent) was a single male.

Table 14. Prior Adoption Experience*

Prior Adoption Experience	Number	Percent
No	88	86%
Yes, second adoption	9	9%
Yes, third adoption	3	3%
Yes, fourth adoption	1	1%
Not able to determine from interview	1	1%
Total	**102**	**100%**

*Percentages are calculated on the total number of discontinued families (n = 102).

Table 15. Family Race/Ethnicity*

Race/Ethnicity	Number	Percent
Caucasian (non-Hispanic)	68	69%
African American	15	15%
Interracial	9	9%
Hispanic	3	3%
Mixed race/ethnicity	2	2%
Native American	1	1%
Asian	0	0%
Total**	**98**	**100%**

*Percentages are calculated on the total number of finalized families (n = 98).
**Percentages do not always add to 100% due to rounding.

Table 16. Family Structure*

Family Structure	Number	Percent
Married couples	60	61%
Unmarried couples-same sex	7	7%
Unmarried couples-opposite sex	1	1%
Single females	29	30%
Single males	1	1%
Total	**98**	**100%**

*Percentages are calculated on the total number of finalized families (n = 98).

d. Type of Adoption

Of the 98 finalized families in the Barriers study, the majority (n = 87, 89 percent) were general adopters. Seven families (seven percent) adopted a child they were fostering, three families (three percent) adopted a specific child with whom they were acquainted, and one family (one percent) adopted a child who was a relative.

A comparison of characteristics of families who discontinued the adoption process and families who completed the adoption process revealed that there were no statistically significant differences between the two samples on any of the above "type of adoption" variables: general adoption, foster adoption, child specific (non-relative) adoption, and relative/kin adoption.

Table 17. Type of Adoption*

Type of Adoption	Number	Percent
General adoption	87	89%
Foster adoption	7	7%
Child specific adoption (non-relative)	3	3%
Relative/Kin adoption	1	1%
Total	**98**	**100%**

*Percentages are calculated on the total number of finalized families (n = 98).

7. Motivation to Adopt through Foster Care

This section discusses the data related to this study's fifth research question: are there differences in motivation for adoption between families who completed the process and those who discontinued the process.

Study participants were asked why they chose to adopt a child with special needs through the foster care system rather than completing a private infant adoption or seeking an international adoption. Responses were similar among finalized (n = 98) and discontinued (n = 102) families. The five most common responses were: "wanted to help a disadvantaged child/child with special needs/child waiting in foster care" [n = 45 (46 percent) finalized and n = 42 (41 percent) discontinued]; "financial reasons – too expensive to do private or international" [n = 39 (40 percent) finalized and n = 35 (34 percent) discontinued]; "didn't want a baby" [n = 25 (26 percent) finalized and n = 22 (22 percent) discontinued]; "wanted an older child" [n = 17 (17 percent) finalized and n = 24 (24 percent) discontinued]; and "there are so many children in the U.S. that I do not want to do an international adoption" [n = 25 (26 percent) finalized and n = 14 (14 percent) discontinued].

8. Demographic Characteristics of Adopted Children

This section discusses the data related to this study's sixth research question: what are the characteristics of children adopted by families who completed the process.

In this study, 98 families completed the adoption process, received children, and finalized their adoptions. A total of 158 children were adopted by these families. Twenty-two adopted children (14 percent) were less than one year old; 62 children (39 percent) were between one and five years old; 48 children (30 percent) were between six and 10 years old; 18 children (11 percent) were between 11 and 13 years old; and eight children (five percent) were 14 years or older. Just over half (n = 81, 51 percent) were female, while 75 children (47 percent) were male. Gender data for two children (one percent) were missing. Sixty children (38 percent) were Caucasian, 38 children (24 percent) were biracial, 28 children (18 percent) were African American, and 18 children (11 percent) were Hispanic. Race/ethnicity data for 14 children (nine percent) were missing. One hundred thirty-nine children (88 percent) were part of a sibling group.

The most challenging child issues known by the adoptive families at placement were medical needs (n = 34, 22 percent); history of abuse and neglect prior to adoption (n = 34, 22 percent); ADD/ADHD (n = 29, 18 percent); educational needs (n = 26, 16 percent); behavioral problems (n = 22, 14 percent); and prenatal drug or alcohol exposure (n = 22, 14 percent).

9. Demographic Characteristics of the Children Whose Adoptive Placements Disrupted

This section discusses the data related to this study's seventh research question: what are the characteristics of children placed with the prospective adoptive families, but whose placements disrupted before finalization.

Seventeen of the 102 discontinued families (17 percent) had children placed with them for adoption, but those placements later disrupted and the families discontinued their plans to adopt. A total of 19 children were placed with these 17 families. Three children (16 percent) were less than one year old; three children (16 percent) were between one and five years old; eight children (42 percent) were between six and 10 years old; three children (16 percent) were between 11 and 13 years; and two children (11 percent) were 14 years or older. Twelve children (63 percent) were female, and seven children (37 percent) were male. Nine children (47 percent) were Caucasian, one child (five percent) was African American, one child (five percent) was Hispanic, and two children (11 percent) were biracial. Ethnic background data for six children (32 percent) were missing. Nine children (47 percent) were part of a sibling group.[11]

The most challenging child issues known by prospective adoptive families at placement of these children were ADD/ADHD (n = five, 26 percent); medical needs (n = four, 21 percent); behavioral problems (n = three, 16 percent); and educational needs (n = three, 16 percent). Additional issues at the point of disruption, which were not known to the prospective adoptive parents at placement, included: developmental/cognitive delays or mental retardation (n = six, 32 percent); mental/emotional health or difficulty controlling emotions (n = five, 26 percent); physical aggression (n = five, 26 percent);

history as a victim of sexual abuse (n = four, 21 percent); and lack of ability to attach appropriately (n = four, 21 percent).

B. Barriers for Adoptive Parents

This section discusses the data related to the eighth and ninth research questions: in which parts of the adoption process do prospective adoptive parents encounter the most barriers, and what are the most frequent barriers they encounter at different stages of the process.

1. Process Group Categories and Steps in the Adoption Process

After in-depth analyses of the interview transcripts of the 200 (102 finalized and 98 discontinued) families, the participants were divided into the following five groups based on the steps in the adoption process they had completed:

1) Families who made an initial contact with an agency, may have attended orientation, and started or completed their initial application, but then discontinued the adoption process;
2) Families who had completed an application, but discontinued the adoption process prior to approval, during either the training or home study process;
3) Families who completed their home study and training, were approved, but never had a child placed with them;
4) Families with whom a child was placed, but the adoption disrupted prior to finalization and the family subsequently discontinued the adoption process; and
5) Families who completed the adoption process, received a child, and finalized the adoption.

2. Barriers Coding and Analysis Methodology

The families' experiences with the adoption process were coded to assess child, family, and agency barriers that each group of families experienced. Coders read the transcript and identified every barrier that families felt impacted their entire adoption process. These barriers for the five family groups are discussed in the "Overall Barriers" sections below. After identifying the overall barriers, coders then narrowed the list of barriers to those that appeared to most negatively impact the families' adoption process. These barriers are discussed below for the five family groups in the section "Top Barriers."

Table 18. Steps Completed in Adoption Process*

Steps Completed	Discontinued Families	Finalized Families	Total
Group 1: Initial contact, orientation, and/or application	5 (5%)	0 (0%)	5 (3%)
Group 2: Application completed but discontinued prior to approval (during home study or training)	27 (26%)	0 (0%)	27 (14%)
Group 3: Approved, received referral(s) or no referral, no child placed	53 (52%)	0 (0%)	53 (27%)
Group 4: Child placed but no finalization (disrupted placement)	17 (17%)	0 (0%)	17 (9%)
Group 5: Finalized adoption	0	98 (100%)	98 (49%)
Total**	**102**	**98**	**200 (100%)**

*Percentages are calculated on the total for each column (e.g., n = 102 for discontinued families). **Percentages do not always add to 100% due to rounding.

Barrier codes were analyzed and grouped into factors representing related or similar responses.[12] Child factors include child's attachment (child's ability to attach to adoptive family); foster care experiences and history (child's experiences in the birthfamily and foster care, history and length in care); behavior; health; mental health; educational needs; and demographics (e.g., age and race/ethnicity).

Family factors include: family commitment (to child and adoption process); ability to interact with systems (ability to work with child welfare system, school system, etc.); support systems (formal and informal); preparation and expectations (life experiences such as prior adoptions, level of expectations, understanding of type of child available); parent-child match; family composition; family dynamics (e.g., level of functioning prior to adoption application, spousal disagreement); child integration (how completely family accepts child); parenting ability and temperament; change in personal circumstances (change due to relocation, death, illness, unemployment, etc.); and family distress at placement disruption/child no longer available.

Agency factors include: availability of services (e.g., therapy, respite care); agency emotional support (agency encouragement and helpfulness);

availability of financial support (e.g., Medicaid, subsidy); adoption process logistics (e.g., jumping through hoops, red tape); legal system interactions (legal assistance during termination of parental rights (TPR), finalization); jurisdictional and inter-jurisdictional issues (challenges with working with multiple agencies, counties, States); family assessment (agency screening process); level of agency bias and cultural competence; agency communication/responsiveness (worker competence, information sharing and disclosure); and adoption exchange (helpfulness of exchange, worker response to exchange inquiries).

3. Barriers Reported by Families in Different Stages of the Adoption Process

The family data were analyzed to identify barriers that influenced the overall adoption process for each family. Families identified, on average, 10.5 barriers that negatively impacted their adoption process. For each family, the top barriers[13] that had the greatest impact on the family's decision to discontinue the adoption process, or presented the greatest challenges for families who finalized an adoption, were then identified. The top barriers do not represent all of the barriers experienced by a family, but rather those barriers that had the greatest influence on the family and their adoption process. The results within each group reported below indicate first the information on all barriers encountered by families in that group, followed by top barriers that families reported in that group.

Additional statistical analysis were completed to determine if there was any relationship between the types of barriers reported and the family groups.[14] The number of child, family, and agency factors were all statistically significantly related ($p < .05$) to the group assignment for families. Seventy-seven percent of families in Group 4 (disrupted placement) and 40 percent of families in Group 5 (finalized adoption) reported child factors to be overall barriers to their adoption process. All families in Group 1 (discontinued after orientation) and Group 4 (disrupted placement) reported family factors as barriers to their overall adoption process. Fifty percent of Group 5 (finalized adoption) reported family factors as barriers. Families in all five groups reported agency factors as barriers to their overall adoption process: 80 percent of Group 1; 93 percent of Group 2; 100 percent of Group 3; 100 percent of Group 4; and 100 percent of Group 5.

An analysis of variance (ANOVA) was run on the groups to determine if the number of child factors, family factors, and agency factors was related to the family group. Frequencies for each type of factor reported by families were significantly related to the group assignment ($p < .05$). Families in Group 4 (disrupted placement) reported a mean of 4.1 agency factors followed by Group 5 (finalized) who reported a mean of 3.9 agency factors and Group 3 (discontinued after approval) who reported a mean of 3.6 agency factors. Groups 1 and 2 reported less than three agency factors per family, on average.

Family factor barriers were most frequently reported by Groups 1 and 4 with a mean of 2.0 and 2.6 respectively. All other groups reported a mean of less than two family factors per family. Group 4 families (disrupted placement) reported a mean of 1.2 child factors. Groups 1, 2, 3 and 5 all reported a mean of less than one child factor.

A post-hoc analysis was conducted to determine if there were statistically significant differences between groups for each factor type: child, family, and agency. [15] For child factors, the following groups differed significantly in the number of factors reported: Group 1 (discontinued after orientation/ application) and Group 4 (disrupted placement); Group 2 (discontinued during training/home study) and Group 4 (disrupted placement), with Group 4 (disrupted placement) reporting the highest number of child factors on average. For family factors, the following groups differed significantly in the number of factors reported: Group 2 (discontinued during training/home study) and Group 5 (finalized adoption); Group 3 (discontinued after approval) and Group 4 (disrupted placement); Group 3 (discontinued after approval) and Group 5 (finalized adoption); Group 4 (disrupted placement) and Group 5 (finalized adoption), with Group 5 (finalized adoption) reporting the fewest family factors on average. For agency factors, the following groups differed significantly in the number of factors reported: Group 1 (discontinued after orientation/application) and Group 4 (disrupted placement); Group 1 (discontinued after orientation/application) and Group 5 (finalized adoption); Group 2 (discontinued during training/home study) and Group 5 (finalized adoption), with Groups 4 (disrupted placement) and 5 (finalized adoption) respectively reporting the highest number of agency factors on average.

Chi-square test of independence was conducted on the most frequently reported agency factors to determine if there was a relationship between those factors and the family groups. The most frequently reported agency factors were: agency emotional support, adoption process logistics, jurisdictional and inter-jurisdictional issues, and agency responsiveness. All of these factors, except jurisdictional and inter-jurisdictional issues, were significantly related to the family's stage of completion in the adoption process (Groups 1-5).

The jurisdictional and inter-jurisdictional issues factor was equally distributed across the five groups. Agency emotional support was reported by

130 families, 45 percent of which were in Group 5 (finalized adoption) and 31 percent of which were in Group 3 (discontinued after approval). Adoption process logistics was reported by 185 families; 52 percent fell into Group 5 (finalized adoption) and only eight percent in Group 4 (disrupted placement). Of the 159 families reporting agency communication/ responsiveness, 49 percent were in Group 5 and less than one percent was in Group 1. See Table 19 for complete data.

a. Group 1 Families

Five prospective adoptive families made initial contact with the agency, participated in an orientation session, and completed an application before they discontinued the process. Two out of five (40 percent) families in Group 1 worked with private agencies, and three out of five (60 percent) worked with public agencies.

Overall Barriers. When the total number of barriers was analyzed for this group, family factors remained the primary type of barrier that influenced these families' decisions to discontinue the adoption process. Additional family factors included family composition, parent-child match, and family distress at placement disruption/child no longer available. In addition, some families identified agency factors as areas of concern for them. These factors included adoption process logistics, family assessment, agency communication /responsiveness, agency emotional support and availability of financial support.

Top Barriers. All families in this group cited family factors as reasons for discontinuing the adoption process. One family also cited an agency factor. These participants did not cite any child factors as barriers to their adoption process. The family factors included family commitment, family dynamics, change in personal circumstances, and family preparation and expectations. The family who identified an agency factor as influential in their decision to discontinue cited adoption process logistics as a barrier. Specifically, this family was concerned that the process would take too long.

b. Group 2 Families

Twenty-seven prospective adoptive families completed an application to adopt but discontinued prior to finishing the training and/or home study. Ten out of 27 (37 percent) families in Group 2 worked with private agencies and 17 out of 27 (63 percent) families worked with public agencies.

Table 19. Most Frequently Reported Agency Factors*

Family Group	Agency Emotional Support	Adoption Process Logistics	Jurisdictional and Inter-jurisdictional	Agency Communication/ Responsiveness
Group 1 (n = 5) Discontinued after orientation/application	1 (.8%)	3 (1.6%)	0 (0%)	1 (.6%)
Group 2 (n = 27) Discontinued during training/home study	16 (12.3%)	22 (11.9%)	3 (5.8%)	19 (11.9%)
Group 3 (n = 53) Discontinued after approval	40 (30.8%)	50 (27%)	15 (28.8%)	46 (28.9%)
Group 4 (n = 17) Discontinued after disrupted placement	15 (11.5%)	14 (7.6%)	5 (9.6%)	15 (9.4%)
Group 5 (n = 98) Finalized adoption	58 (44.6%)	96 (51.9%)	29 (55.8%)	78 (49.1%)
Total Number of families reporting factor**	**130**	**185**	**52**	**159**

*Percentages are calculated on the total for each column (e.g., n = 130 for parents reporting agency emotional support).

**Percentages do not always add to 100% due to rounding.

Overall Barriers.[16] When all barriers were identified by families in this group, five families (19 percent) reported child factors, 21 families (78 percent) reported family factors, and 25 families (93 percent) reported agency factors. The most frequently reported child factor was child's mental health (11 percent). The most frequently reported family factors were change in personal circumstances (37 percent), followed by parent-child match, family commitment, family composition, family preparation and expectations, and family dynamics, all at 19 percent. For 15 percent of families, parenting ability and temperament was a barrier.

In the overall barriers, the main agency factors were adoption process logistics (81 percent), agency communication/responsiveness (70 percent), agency emotional support (59 percent), and level of agency bias and cultural competence (30 percent). The following quote is illustrative of barriers experienced by families in this group:

"The main barriers are getting social workers to call you back. My son was not on any of the websites. Had he not needed an immediate placement and they placed the call to our agency, I wouldn't have known about it. And the kids that are on the website – it takes forever to get information, to get caseworkers to call back. I mean there are kiddos on there now that were there two years ago when I first started looking. And, you know, you just get no response. I mean there are a lot of kids I've asked about, and you don't get responses."

Top Barriers. The top barriers experienced by families in this group were all family factors (59 percent) or agency factors (63 percent). Change in personal circumstances led 33 percent of the families in this group to discontinue. Examples of these changes included relocation, job change, marital status change, and death/illness in the family. Fifteen percent identified barriers related to family preparation and expectations, including parents' expectations of the children available for adoption. Seven percent cited family dynamics as a barrier. Each of the following three family factors were indicated by four percent of the families in this group as barriers: parenting ability and temperament, family commitment, and family composition. This group reported six agency factors: adoption process logistics (41 percent), agency communication/responsiveness (33 percent), agency emotional support (26 percent), level of agency bias and cultural competence (seven percent), availability of services (four percent), and family assessment (four percent).

c. Group 3 Families

Fifty-three families were approved for adoption but never had a child placed with them and subsequently discontinued the adoption process. Thirty-six out of 53 (68 percent) families in Group 3 worked with private agencies, and 17 out of 53 (32 percent) worked with public agencies.

Overall Barriers. When all barriers mentioned by families in this group were explored, the frequency of barriers reported increased in all factor types: child, family, and agency factors. The most reported child factor was child's foster care experiences and history (26 percent), followed by child's mental health (11 percent) and child's health (eight percent). The most reported family barriers were change in personal circumstances (32 percent), parent-child match (23 percent), family preparation and expectations (21 percent), family commitment (17 percent), and family dynamics (17 percent).

The most often reported agency barriers were adoption process logistics (94 percent), agency communication/responsiveness (87 percent), agency emotional support (75 percent), jurisdictional and inter-jurisdictional issues (28 percent), level of agency bias and cultural competence (28 percent), and availability of services (26 percent). Families discussed their feelings in the following quotes:

> "The waiting for a match was very challenging. And it was gut-wrenching at times because you know your profile is sitting on somebody's desk, and this one person who has never met you before is going to decide if you are right for this child that you know you're right for. And that was the part of the process that's just—I know it's impossible for every caseworker to meet with every parent who's involved with every kid. But for us, we felt like we were just so ready; the waiting and everything being out of our hands was the most gut-wrenching and challenging part of the process."
>
> "We would get calls that would never go further than the initial call. 'We have this child, are you interested ...' and my answer was always, 'yes.' It just never seemed to happen. I guess five or six times they called like that and I said, 'what's the next step?' 'Well, I'll call you back with the details, blah, blah, blah.' But the call back never came."
>
> "Many times – we waited, kept getting put off, then would get a letter saying the child was placed with another family – too emotionally draining. They should do their homework prior to telling you they think they have a match. We were never told why we were not chosen."

Top Barriers: Few families (13 percent) in Group 3 reported child factors to be the top barrier influencing their decision to discontinue. Families in this group primarily reported family factors (53 percent) and agency factors (81 percent) to be the top barriers. The child factors identified as top barriers were foster care experiences and history (six percent) and child's mental health (four percent). Twenty-six percent of the families reported change in personal circumstances as a primary cause of discontinuing the process. Nine percent cited family commitment. The three other most frequently indicated family factors were parent-child match (eight percent), family preparation and expectations (eight percent), and family dynamics (eight percent).

Families in Group 3 also described agency factors that impeded their adoption process. The top four agency factors were adoption process logistics (51 percent), agency responsiveness (49 percent), agency emotional support (42 percent), and jurisdictional and inter-jurisdictional issues (13 percent). One example of a specific difficulty was the frustration families experienced after being referred a child, expressing interest, and then not being chosen for that child, often without being given a reason for the agency's choice.

d. Group 4 Families

The 17 families in this group discontinued the adoption process after a disrupted placement. Eleven out of 17 (65 percent) families who experienced a disrupted placement worked with private agencies, and six out of 17 (35 percent) worked with public agencies.

Overall Barriers. When the total number of barriers was analyzed for this group, the frequency of families reporting barriers increased in all three factor types: child, family, and agency factors. All families in this group (100 percent) identified agency and family barriers. Families identified six child factors, with foster care experiences and history (53 percent) and child's attachment (29 percent) being the most frequently identified. Families again reported nine family factor barriers influencing their decision to discontinue the adoption process, with the most frequently cited barrier being family distress at placement disruption/child no longer available (94 percent), parent-child match (41 percent), family commitment (24 percent), support systems (24 percent), family preparation and expectations (24 percent), and family dynamics (24 percent).

In the overall barriers, families reported nine agency factor barriers. The most frequently reported of the agency factor barriers were agency emotional support (88 percent), agency communication/responsiveness (88 percent), adoption process logistics (82 percent), availability of services (53 percent), jurisdictional and inter-jurisdictional issues (29 percent), level of agency bias and cultural competence (29 percent), and legal system interactions (24 percent).

One example of an agency communication/responsiveness barrier concerns disclosure of information about the child to the adoptive family. Families reported instances of child information being withheld, mis-represented, or potential issues they may encounter in the future being minimized. One family discussed their feelings in the following quote:

> "When it came to reviewing the kids' files and everything, they lied to us. They didn't tell us the problems that these kids were having, and there wasn't anything in their files that we read about—some of the things that we found out later on after we had the kids. You know. None of this. And so, we found out that the little boy had been sexually abused when he was younger

by his grandfather, which we did not know. So we didn't know how to deal with it when it started coming out. That's when we started taking him to get help. But it was probably the worst experience that we've been through in our lives. I don't think we ever want to go through it again."

Top Barriers: Child factors were reported as top barriers by 29 percent of families in Group 4, more than in any other group: child's attachment (12 percent), foster care experiences and history (18 percent), child's behavior (six percent), and child's mental health (six percent). Nine family barrier factors were reported as top barriers in this group. Five factors were reported by 10 percent or more families: family distress at placement disruption/child no longer available (65 percent), parent-child match (18 percent), family commitment (12 percent), family dynamics (12 percent), and child integration (12 percent).

Families in this group reported eight agency factors as top barriers. They were level of agency emotional support (71 percent), agency Communication /responsiveness (47 percent), adoption process logistics (41 percent), availability of services (29 percent), level of agency bias and cultural competence (18 percent), legal system interactions (18 percent), jurisdictional and inter-jurisdictional issues (18 percent), and family assessment (six percent).

e. Group 5 Families

The 98 families in this group finalized an adoption. Fifty-six out of 98 (57 percent) finalized families worked with private agencies, and 42 out of 98 (43 percent) families worked with public agencies.

Overall Barriers. When the total number of barriers was analyzed for families in Group 5, the frequency of families reporting barriers increased in all factor types: child, family, and agency factors. The most frequently reported child factors were foster care experiences and history (26 percent) and child's behavior (14 percent). The most frequently reported family factors were family commitment (18 percent), family preparation and expectations (15 percent), and family composition (10 percent).

In the overall barriers, the families reported ten agency factors. The most frequently reported were adoption process logistics (98 percent), agency communication/responsiveness (80 percent), agency emotional support (59 percent), availability of services (39 percent), jurisdictional and inter-jurisdictional issues (30 percent), legal system interactions (27 percent), and level of agency bias and cultural competence (22 percent).

Top Barriers. Although these families completed the adoption process, they still identified barriers encountered in the adoption process. Specifically, they reported five top child factors, eight top family factors, and ten top agency factors that were barriers to their process. The most frequently reported top child factors were child's foster care experiences and history (six percent) and child's behaviors (six percent). Of the top family factors, the most reported were family preparation and expectations (nine percent), family commitment (six percent), family composition (four percent), and child integration (four percent).

Families in Group 5 most frequently reported agency factors as the top barriers in their adoption process. The most frequently identified top agency factors were adoption process logistics (68 percent), agency communication /responsiveness (46 percent), agency emotional support (23 percent), availability of services (15 percent), jurisdictional and inter-jurisdictional issues (14 percent), legal system interactions (11 percent), and level of agency bias and cultural competence (10 percent). Examples of services needed included therapy, support groups, and psychiatric services.

4. Summary of Adoption Barriers

- Families in Group 1 who discontinued very early in the process reported that family factors were most influential in their decision to discontinue the adoption process.
- Families who finalized an adoption (Group 5) were less likely to report family barriers than families in Groups 1-4 (all families who discontinued the process of adopting a child from foster care) when barriers were analyzed overall, as well as when barriers were analyzed for the top barriers that led them to discontinue.
- Families in Group 4 (disrupted placement) experienced the highest frequency of child barrier factors (76 percent), but only 29 percent of the families in this group reported child factors to be among the top barriers that influenced their decision to discontinue the process of adopting a child from foster care.
- Families who finalized an adoption (Group 5) or discontinued after a disrupted placement (Group 4) reported the most agency barriers. Ninety-eight percent of the 98 families who had finalized adoptions

and 82 percent of the 17 families with a disrupted placement identified adoption process logistics as an agency barrier factor. A trend emerges that indicates this factor is reported by more families as they move further along in the adoption process: Group 1 = 60 percent, Group 2 = 81 percent, Group 3 = 94 percent, Group 4 = 82 percent, and Group 5 = 98 percent. When analyzing the prevalence of the factor as a top barrier, a similar trend emerges: Group 1 = 20 percent, Group 2 = 41 percent, Group 3 = 51 percent, Group 4 = 41 percent, and Group 5 = 68 percent.

- Families who discontinued the adoption process after approval or after a disrupted placement and families who finalized an adoption from foster care (Groups 3-5) reported the highest number of agency barriers overall. Families who finalized an adoption (Group 5) reported the highest number of agency barriers as top barriers in their adoption process.

5. Barriers to Adoption Experienced by Families of Color and Caucasian Families

This section discusses the data related to this study's tenth research question: were there differences between families of color and Caucasian families in their identification of barriers to adoption.

To assess whether there were any differences in barriers to adoption between families of color and Caucasian families, the two types of families in each of the five adoption process groups were compared on all child, family, and agency factor barriers. For families who finalized an adoption of a child from foster care, there were no statistically significant differences between families of color and Caucasian families on any of the factors.

However, differences were found among families who discontinued the adoption process. When analyzing the ***top barriers*** reported by families who discontinued the adoption process, there were statistically significant differences ($p = .05$) between families of color and Caucasian families on one family factor, family dynamics (e.g., level of functioning prior to adoption application, and spousal disagreement), and one agency factor, jurisdictional and inter- jurisdictional issues (challenges with working with multiple agencies, counties, States). As barriers, families of color were more likely to report the family factor, family dynamics, (19 percent v. four percent) and Caucasian families were more likely to report the agency barrier, jurisdictional and inter-jurisdictional issues (14 percent v. 0 percent).

In an analysis of the ***overall barriers*** impacting the adoption process for families who discontinued, there were also statistically significant differences ($p = .05$) between families of color and Caucasian families on two family factors (family distress at placement disruption/child no longer available and change in personal circumstances) and one agency factor (jurisdictional and inter-jurisdictional issues). Caucasian families were more likely to report the family factor, family distress at placement disruption/child no longer available (24 percent v. seven percent), and families of color were more likely to report the family factor, change in personal circumstances (change due to relocation, death, illness, unemployment, etc.) (42 percent v. 23 percent). Caucasian families were more likely to report the agency barrier, jurisdictional and inter-jurisdictional issues (30 percent v. seven percent).

When analyzing the ***top barriers*** reported by families who discontinued the adoption process, families of color were more likely to report the family factor, family dynamics (19 percent v. four percent), and Caucasian families were more likely to report the agency barrier, jurisdictional and inter-jurisdictional issues (14 percent v. 0 percent). In an analysis of the ***overall barriers*** impacting the adoption process for families who discontinued, Caucasian families were more likely to report the family factor, family distress at placement disruption/child no longer available (24 percent v. seven percent), whereas families of color were more likely to report the family factor, change in personal circumstances (change due to relocation, death, illness, unemployment, etc.) (42 percent v. 23 percent). Caucasian families were more likely to report the agency barrier, jurisdictional and inter-jurisdictional issues (30 percent v. seven percent).

IV. Study 1

Barriers Study: Staff Perspectives

A. Methods

To obtain additional perspectives on barriers to adoption, the research team distributed surveys to participating public and private agencies for completion by administrative staff, recruitment staff, adoption exchange staff, adoption subsidy staff, and family and child workers. A goal of 360 completed staff surveys was set. The 29 items on the survey included questions assessing agency and system barriers, family and child barriers, solutions to overcome barriers, and child's preparation for adoption. The survey was available to agencies in either electronic or hard copy form. Electronic copies were sent to agency liaisons via e-mail attachments and liaisons were asked to forward the survey to all available adoption-related staff for completion. Hard copies were mailed in individual packets to agency liaisons and individual packets were provided to all available adoption-related staff. Both versions of the survey were sent with a cover letter, which contained instructions for completing and returning the survey. Hard copy surveys were also distributed at national, regional, and local conferences and trainings by the Principal Investigator or AdoptUsKids Trainers.

Table 20. Barriers Experienced by Families of Color and Caucasian Families*

Overall Barrier Comparison for Families with Discontinued Adoptions (n = 102)	Was a Barrier	Families of Color (n = 31)		Caucasian Families (n = 71)		Total (n = 102)	
Family distress at placement disruption/Child no longer available**	No	29	93%	54	76%	83	81%
	Yes	2	7%	17	24%	19	19%
Change in personal circumstances**	No	18	58%	55	77%	73	72%
	Yes	13	42%	16	23%	29	28%
Jurisdictional and inter-jurisdictional issues**	No	29	93%	50	70%	79	77%
	Yes	2	7%	21	30%	23	23%
Top Barrier Comparison For Families with Discontinued Adoptions (n = 101*)**	**Was a barrier**	**Families of Color (n = 31)**		**Caucasian Families (n = 70)**		**Total (n = 101)**	
Family dynamics**	No	25	81%	67	96%	92	91%
	Yes	6	19%	3	4%	9	9%
Jurisdictional and inter-jurisdictional issues**	No	31	100%	60	86%	91	90%
	Yes	0	0%	10	14%	10	10%

*Percentages are calculated for each factor by the family's ethnicity (e.g., n = 31families of color).

** $p < .05$

***One family did not report any family barriers in the "top barrier" analysis, so they are not represented in this sample.

Approximately 1,659 surveys were sent to staff in 34 States and Washington, D.C. A total of 382 (23 percent) surveys were returned. Surveys were returned from staff located in 29 States and the District of Columbia.[17]

B. Staff Demographics

Of the 382 respondents, 323 (85 percent) were female, 39 (10 percent) were male, and 20 (five percent) did not provide information about their gender. On average, staff respondents had worked at their current agency 10.3 years. Two hundred sixty-nine staff (70 percent) worked in a State agency, and 113 (30 percent) worked in a private agency.

C. Results

From a list of agency, family, and child factors, staff respondents were asked to rate on a scale of one to five the extent to which they believed these factors were barriers to the adoption process, with "one" indicating "not a barrier at all" and "five" indicating a "major barrier." For purposes of analysis, ratings of two and three were combined to indicate "somewhat a barrier" and responses four and five were combined to indicate "major barrier." The top five agency, family, and child factors rated by staff as "major barriers" are described below. Additional analyses were conducted on the seven States with public and private agency representation (59 private agency staff and 78 public agency staff) to determine whether statistically significant differences existed between public and private agency staff members' perceptions of major agency, family, and child barriers, using a significance level of .05. Unless otherwise noted, statistically significant differences were not found between public and private agency staff perceptions of major barriers.

1. Agency Barriers

1. Inadequate pool of families appropriate for adoption of children with special needs/Inadequate pool of prospective adoptive families (in general)

Of the 382 staff respondents, 67 percent (n = 255) rated "inadequate pool of families appropriate for adoption of children with special needs" as a major barrier (rated a four or five on the rating scale). Fifty percent also rated "inadequate pool of prospective adoptive families (in general)" as a major barrier.

After rating each factor listed on the survey on a scale from one to five, survey respondents were given an opportunity to identify strategies for overcoming the factors they rated as "major barriers." For example, to overcome the problem of having an inadequate pool of prospective adoptive families, the majority of respondents Stated that agencies should increase their efforts at family recruitment. More specifically, staff noted that "recruitment of minority families" and "families willing to adopt older children and sibling groups" were needed. Other solutions to this barrier included: 1) hiring workers whose sole responsibility is recruitment; 2) improving and increasing marketing and community awareness; and 3) dedicating State funds to Statewide recruitment. One respondent also added that agencies should "utilize our families to get the word out about adopting," as [adoptive] families are "a major resource we have yet to use."

There was a statistically significant difference in how public and private agency adoption staff perceived barriers related to inadequate pools of families, in general and for children with special needs. Analyses revealed that 60 percent of adoption staff working in private agencies rated "the lack of families appropriate for adoption of special needs children" as a major barrier, whereas 80 percent of adoption staff in public agencies rated it as a major barrier.

2. Jurisdictional issues related to termination of parental rights (publication, litigation, full dockets, etc.)

Forty-eight percent (n = 183) of survey respondents rated "jurisdictional issues related to termination of parental rights (TPR)" as a major barrier. Full dockets, paperwork delays, too few judges and court personnel, appeals by birthparents, and judges giving birthparents "too many chances" were all cited as reasons for delays in the termination process. Over half (59 percent) of respondents who rated this a major barrier believed that hiring more judges and attorneys and training and educating judges and attorneys, specifically about the Child Protective Service system and termination of parental rights, would begin to address this barrier. Other solutions offered by respondents included changing current laws and policies to speed up the process, prioritizing TPR cases, increasing communication and cooperation within the jurisdictions, and reducing caseloads or hiring more staff to address the problem of paperwork delays.

3. Interstate Compact on the Placement of Children (ICPC)

Of 382 staff respondents, 46 percent (n = 176) believed that there were barriers in relation to the Interstate Compact on the Placement of Children (ICPC). Poor communication and coordination between States, failure to adhere to timelines, and disagreement between States regarding responsibility for services were all cited as problematic aspects of the ICPC process. One respondent characterized the ICPC process as a "large barrier for out-of-State adoptions... Once a family is selected in another State and the ICPC application has been processed, the child CANNOT visit the selected family. Time to bond must be put on hold; often the process takes six to nine months to get approval in the receiving State."

Solutions that were suggested by staff to overcome barriers related to ICPC included streamlining the entire process, holding States accountable for ICPC timelines and service provision, and promoting cooperation among workers while also emphasizing worker persistence. One staff member specifically suggested that "bureaucratic barriers" to the ICPC process be reduced by "hold[ing] States accountable for delays in completing home studies or approving placement, [and] eliminating discrepancies between IV-E Medical Assistance and non-IV-E Medical Assistance for kids moving across State lines."[18]

There was a statistically significant difference in how public and private agency adoption staff perceived ICPC barriers. Analyses revealed that 34 percent of adoption staff in private agencies rated ICPC as a major barrier, whereas 64 percent of adoption staff in public agencies rated it as a major barrier.

4. Size of workers' caseloads

Forty-five percent (n = 172) of survey respondents rated "size of workers' caseloads" as a major barrier to the successful completion of the adoption process. For many caseworkers, this not only included the number of cases carried but also a number and range of responsibilities in areas other than adoption, such as child protection. Both were thought to create delays in the adoption process.

Of the respondents who listed caseload size as a major barrier, 62 percent said the solution to this problem was to reduce caseloads by hiring more staff. In addition, respondents believed that worker responsibilities needed to be reorganized or reduced in order to increase their focus on adoption cases. They believed that hiring more workers might also help to relieve some of the additional responsibilities that they have. Respondents suggested that in order to hire and retain competent and committed staff, agencies should increase pay as well as provide compensatory and overtime pay.

There was a statistically significant difference in how public and private agency adoption staff perceived caseload barriers. Analyses revealed that 42 percent of adoption staff in private agencies rated caseload size as a major barrier, whereas 63 percent of adoption staff in public agencies rated it as a major barrier.

5. Availability of post-adoption services after finalization/Lack of respite care

Forty-two percent (n = 160) of survey respondents believed that the lack of availability of post-adoption services after finalization was a major barrier in the adoption process. Services seemed to be particularly scarce in rural areas. One respondent noted the "limited availability of services for children with serious special needs, especially in the area of mental health and sexual abuse." Forty percent also rated the lack of respite care services as a major barrier.

More than half (56 percent) of respondents who rated lack of post-adoption services as a major barrier believed that funding was the best solution to this problem. While some respondents noted that existing services should be improved, most concluded that existing services could be expanded and improved through funding, and that new services could be offered if more funding was available. One respondent proposed that prospective adoptive families provide respite for families who have adopted, which would provide a needed service for adoptive families, and serve the purpose of providing the hands-on training that respondents believed to be critical in several areas of family training and education.

2. Family Barriers

1. Prospective adoptive parents' specificity in type of child desired (i.e., parent wants young child with minimal special needs)

Sixty-seven percent (n = 256) of agency staff survey respondents rated the adoptive parents' specificity in the type of child they desired to adopt as a major barrier to the adoption process. Survey responses indicated that prospective adoptive parents may have unrealistic expectations about the type of children available for adoption or unrealistic behavioral expectations of children with special needs. Furthermore, responses seemed to indicate that many prospective adoptive parents want to adopt a young, Caucasian child with minimal special needs.

Of the respondents who rated this as a major barrier, 49 percent believed that the barrier could be overcome through training and education of prospective adoptive parents, as well as hands-on experience with children who have been in foster care. Related to the idea of hands-on experience, one staff member added that "nurturing the relationship between the adoptive parent and former foster parent can be very helpful in helping adoptive families broaden their perspectives on the needs of the child and how community resources can be very helpful." Additional suggestions to overcome this barrier included recruiting families who are open to adopting older children, sibling groups, and children of color, and improving the screening process of prospective adoptive parents. Respondents recommended that agency staff members screen families more rigorously and get more information from prospective parents in the screening process, suggesting that careful and thorough screening early on may reveal prospective parents' desires and expectations and areas in which training and education were needed. Beyond better screening, survey respondents believed that workers have a responsibility to give prospective adoptive families accurate, honest, and thorough information about the type of children who are available for adoption.

2. Prospective adoptive parents' criminal background (major offenses, such as crimes against a person or substance abuse convictions)

Fifty-one percent (n = 195) of survey respondents rated the criminal background of prospective adoptive parents as a major barrier to families being approved for adoption and completing the adoption process. Specifically, offenses such as crimes against a person and substance abuse convictions tended to keep many families from being approved for adoption.

Of the 51 percent who rated criminal background problems as major barriers, 28 percent of survey respondents reported that the barrier should not be overcome or the barrier could not be overcome. Staff also recommended that prospective adoptive parents should be better screened and that criminal and background checks should be thorough and conducted as early as possible.

3. Prospective adoptive parents' inability or unwillingness to accept certain characteristics in a child's history or background

Forty-five percent (n = 172) of staff survey respondents rated prospective adoptive parents' inability or unwillingness to accept certain characteristics of a child's history or background as a major barrier. Some staff members perceive that parents' unwillingness to accept a child's background is due to a lack of education and misunderstanding that "love will solve the problem." Other survey respondents reported that some parents expect children to adapt to their home environment, rather than parents and children adapting and changing together.

Almost two-thirds (64 percent) of respondents who rated this factor as a major barrier suggested that prospective adoptive families should be offered training and education which "stretches" families' perceptions of what types of children and behaviors they can handle. Related to training and education, respondents suggested that training in the form of hands- on experience with children who have lived in foster care would be beneficial. Agency support and family therapy were also offered as ideas for increasing families' acceptance of children's backgrounds and histories.

There was a statistically significant difference in how public and private agency adoption staff perceived barriers related to prospective parents' inability or unwillingness to accept certain child background and history characteristics. Analyses revealed that 41 percent of adoption staff in private agencies rated this as a major barrier, whereas 61 percent of adoption staff in public agencies rated it as a major barrier.

4. Prospective adoptive parents' unwillingness to access services or community resources

Forty-four percent (n = 168) of staff survey respondents rated prospective adoptive parents' unwillingness to access services or community resources as a major barrier to the completion of the adoption process.

Of the 44 percent who rated this factor as a major barrier, 45 percent believed that family training and education were needed to overcome this barrier. Specifically, families needed to be educated on services and resources available in the community, and they needed to be trained on how to access these services and resources. One survey respondent added the following:

"It should be known that our children need safe, stable, loving parents and environments; needing parents who are assertive and who can get the child's needs met if/as they arise. They need parents who are mentally and physically healthy so there is a probability of longer term permanence for the child."

Some adoption staff believed that in addition to training and educating families, more services and resources were needed in the community. In addition, the existing services and resources available in the community should be improved and better funded, namely in the areas of agency support services and family therapy.

5. Prospective adoptive parents' lack of experience with special needs children

Forty-one (n = 157) percent of staff survey respondents perceived prospective parents' lack of experience with special needs children to be a major barrier to the adoption process. Over half (53 percent) of these respondents recommended training and education to overcome this barrier. Twenty-one percent also recommended that family training include hands-on experience with children who have lived in foster care or that families be matched with an adoptive family that can serve as a "mentor" for the prospective family. Adoption staff believed that close supervision and support by the agency would be helpful, as would therapy for the family and adopted child.

3. Child Barriers

1. Child's age

A large majority of survey respondents reported that a child's age (11 years old or older) was a major barrier to the adoption process. Eighty-four percent (n = 321) rated "14 or older" as a major barrier, and 54 percent (n = 206) rated "11 - 13 years old" as a major barrier. One respondent expressed the following sentiment: "We leave kids in inadequate foster homes for too long and let kids get too old in the system. We have no budget for special needs adoption recruitment, even though we know we have hundreds of waiting kids."

When asked to suggest ideas for overcoming barriers related to age, just over half (51 percent) of respondents who rated these to be major barriers thought that recruitment was the solution to age barriers. Respondents reported that recruitment efforts should be targeted and focused on families who are willing to adopt older children. Staff members recognized that the agency's role in overcoming age barriers not only involved recruitment but also increasing community awareness and use of media campaigns. Furthermore, some respondents believed additional family training and education about older children in the system might result in more families considering adoption of an older child. One respondent suggested that agencies and workers "increase the push for parents to adopt teens – end this cycle within systems that says teenagers are unadoptable and don't need families." Another added that agencies should "provide child-specific recruitment efforts to adolescents to locate resources who had an established connection with youth (birth family member, previous foster parent, mentor, coach, teacher, etc.)."

2. Child is currently engaging in sexual perpetrating behaviors/Child has a history of sexual perpetration

The majority of adoption staff who responded to the survey rated "child's current sexual perpetrating behaviors" and "child's history of sexual perpetration" as major barriers to the adoption process (n = 309, 81 percent and n = 294, 77 percent respectively). Workers noted that a lack of adequate therapeutic services to address sexual perpetration issues further compounded this barrier, as did prospective adoptive parents' fears that adopting a child with sexual perpetration issues would harm or negatively impact other children living in their homes.

Of survey respondents who rated sexual perpetration issues as major barriers, 46 percent believed that funding for therapy and support group services for the child and for families was critically needed during pre- and post-adoption. Some workers stated that these services already existed, but that the services would be improved by having therapists who were specifically trained to work with children and families and who could address problems and issues that are unique to adopted children and adoptive families. In addition, adoption staff believed that prospective adoptive parents could benefit from additional training and education, specifically on sexual perpetration issues and handling associated behavioral issues. Five percent of workers believed that children who have histories of being sexual perpetrators or who continue to be sexual perpetrators should not be placed in homes with other children.

3. Child is currently engaging in sexually acting out behaviors/Child has a history of sexual acting out (i.e. public masturbation, provocative, etc.)

Children currently engaging in sexually acting out behaviors or children with histories of sexual acting out were both rated by survey respondents to be major barriers (n = 298, 78 percent and n = 283, 74 percent respectively). Similar to barriers related to sexual perpetration, workers noted that the lack of services, funding for services, and adequate therapeutic services made these barriers even more problematic.

Suggestions for overcoming these barriers were similar to those suggested to address sexual perpetration issues, with the exception of placement with no other children. Again, survey respondents reported a need for funding to create new services for children and families, as well as a need to improve existing services. Family training and education on special needs and behavioral issues of children were also provided as ideas to address sexual acting out issues.

4. Need for siblings to be placed together (group of three or more)

Fifty-six percent (n = 213) of survey respondents reported that sibling groups of three or more needing to be placed together was a major barrier to placement, due to the overall inadequate pool of prospective adoptive families and because of some prospective adoptive families' unwillingness or inability to adopt a sibling group of this size.

Respondents who rated this as a barrier stated that the problem may be overcome by recruiting families who wish or are willing to adopt a sibling group of this size. It also may be addressed by educating current families on the importance of keeping sibling groups together, so that families may broaden their conceptions of what types of children, and how many children, they wish to adopt or can handle.

5. Child has behavior problems in the home

Fifty percent of staff survey respondents reported that children's behavior problems in the home were major barriers in the adoption process. Among the problems mentioned by staff were oppositional defiant behavior, verbal and physical aggression, manipulation, and lying.

Of the 50 percent who rated behavioral problems in the home as a major barrier, 33 percent believed that support and therapy for both the child and the family was necessary to overcome this barrier. Beyond availability of therapy, staff members believed that the quality of the therapeutic services was equally if not more important. One staff member elaborated by saying children should be enrolled in "...positive counseling, not just someone who the kids can bowl over with their stories of abuse and neglect, someone who will get in there and work with the children." Other ideas for overcoming this barrier included training and education for families, particularly in the area of behavioral issues and special needs. Staff members also believed that improved parenting in the form of increased supervision, consistency, and discipline, may be helpful in reducing behavior problems in the home.

4. Differences between Public and Private Agency Staff Perspectives

Differences were noted in perspectives between public and private agency respondents. Adoption staff working in private agencies and public agencies identified agency or administrative, family, and child factors that they perceived to be major barriers to the successful completion of the adoption process. Statistically significant differences existed between public and private agency staffs' perceptions of major agency and family barriers. Although public and private agency staff agreed that the lack of families available and appropriate to adopt children with special needs was a major barrier, public agency staff believed this to be a greater barrier than did private agency staff. Public and private agency staff also differed in how they perceived ICPC and caseload size as major barriers, with public agency staff rating these as greater barriers than private agency staff. In the rating of family barriers, more public agency staff rated the prospective adoptive parents' inability or unwillingness to accept a child's background and history as a major barrier than did staff working in private agencies.

V. STUDY 2

Success Factors Study: Methods and Demographics

A. Methods

As part of The Collaboration to AdoptUsKids, researchers at the University of Texas at Austin conducted a 4-year prospective examination of a nationwide sample of successful adoptive families who adopted children with special needs. Successful adoptive families were defined as families whose finalized adoptions remained intact and the adoptive parents remained committed to parenting the adopted child. A nationwide sample of public and private adoption agencies were asked to assist in identifying adoptive families for participation in the study. Special attention was placed on including families who had adopted older children (particularly between the ages of 12 and 16 years), sibling groups, and children who had been in the foster care system for several years, in order to glean information on how these families and children were adjusting and what factors contributed to positive outcomes. In addition, some families were included whose adopted children were under the age of six at the time of placement but had severe special needs. Although all types of adoptions were included in this sample, the majority were general adoptions which were arranged through both public and private agencies. The sample also included single parent, foster parent, and relative adoptions.

Initially adoption agency staff mailed a "family packet" to adoptive families qualifying for participation. As families submitted completed "packets" to the project office, one adopted child from the family was selected as the "focus child" for the family. The focus child was selected on a case-by-case basis after reviewing the demographic information provided by the adoptive parents. Criteria used to determine the focus child included the age of the child at placement, quality and severity of the child's special needs, level of challenge the child presented to the parents, and length of time the child had been in the adoptive home. The final study sample consisted of 161 families who had adopted at least one child who had been in the home between 1 and 14 years at the time of participation in the study.

Telephone interviews (usually lasting two to three hours) were conducted with one adoptive parent per family using a semi-structured interview schedule. Many interviews lasted longer than three hours, as the adoptive parents seemed to love talking about their families. Topics covered in the interviews included: 1) adoptive parent background and adoption process; 2) couple's relationship at the time of the adoption; 3) child's history and background experiences in foster care; 4) child preparation for adoption and the adoption process; 5) family and child adjustment at the time of the adoption; 6) current adjustment to the adoption and adoptive parent feelings about the child; 7) bonding/attachment/relationship with child; 8) post-adoption services; 9) preparation for ongoing contact with birth family members; and 10) transracial adoption experiences (if applicable). These interviews were tape recorded and transcribed verbatim. Due to the complex nature of these adoptive parent interviews, all interviewers were members of the Collaboration to AdoptUsKids core research team. Interview transcripts of the entire sample of success factors families (N = 161) were double coded by experienced staff members of the AdoptUsKids research team.

In addition to the interview, adoptive families also completed the following survey measure as part of the study. Follow-up surveys were also sent one and two years after the interview.

1. Adoptive Parent Survey

Two weeks after the completion of the telephone interviews, an adoptive parent survey was mailed to participating families. Permission was obtained from Reilly & Platz (2003) who had conducted a similar study of successful special needs adoptions, to adapt, for the purposes of this study, selected questions on the adoptive parents' knowledge of the child's background and history as well as the child's medical, physical, and behavioral challenges. These items were included in the mailed survey in addition to the following two measures:

a. Parenting Stress Inventory (PSI)

The Parenting Stress Inventory (PSI) (Abidin, 1986) is a self-report questionnaire designed to predict a child's current behavioral and emotional adjustment as well as to identify parental stress that may be a function of the parent-child system. The PSI identifies two domains as sources of stressors—child characteristics and parent characteristics. Test-retest reliability ranges from 0.61 for the child domain to 0.91 for the mother domain (Abidin, 1986). The PSI has been normed on both non-clinical and clinical samples of parents. The full version of the PSI consists of 120 items and takes less than 30 minutes to complete. The PSI short form consists of 36 items and results in a Total Stress Score from three scales: Parental Distress, Parent-Child Dysfunctional Interaction, and Difficult Child.

b. Marital Satisfaction Scale

The Marital Satisfaction Scale is a five-item scale assessing marital satisfaction based on the conceptual framework developed by Fowers & Olson (1993) for use in the *ENRICH Marital Satisfaction Scale.*

2. Longitudinal Follow-up Surveys

One and two years after the initial interview, the research team sent follow-up surveys to assess changes in family and child functioning over time.

B. Demographic Characteristics of Successful Families

1. Family Structure: Initial Data Collection

There were 161 families, a total of 270 individual adoptive parents, who participated in the study. The majority of the families (n = 104, 65 percent) were married couples. There were also two unmarried same-sex couples (one percent) and three unmarried opposite-sex couples (two percent). Forty-seven single female adopters composed 29 percent of the sample, and single males represented five of all adoptive parents (three percent).

2. Age, Family Income, and Education

At the time of data collection, the average age of the adoptive mothers was 45 years and adoptive fathers was 46 years. The adoptive families had an average income of $61,991. The average income of the couples was $72,826; single females was $36,922; and single males was $52,800. More than half of the sample of adoptive parents had completed either a bachelor's or graduate degree. Below is a detailed description of the parents' educational levels.

3. Family Race/Ethnicity

The majority of families (n = 128, 80 percent) identified their ethnic background as Caucasian. Eighteen families (11 percent) were African American and five (three percent) were Hispanic. In this sample, there were nine interracial couples (six percent) including Caucasian and African American, African American and Hispanic, Hispanic and Native American, etc. One family (one percent) was of mixed race/ethnicity (e.g., both participants were Caucasian and African American).

4. Transracial and Same-race Adoptive Families: Family and Focus Child Race/Ethnicity

Overall, the majority of families (n = 105, 65 percent) adopted children of the same ethnic background as one parent (n = 8, five percent) or both parents (n = 97, 60 percent): 78 Caucasian (non-Hispanic) (48 percent), 14 African American (nine percent), and five Hispanic (three percent). However, 56 families (35 percent) transracially adopted. Of the transracial adopters, the majority were Caucasian families (n = 50, 89 percent) who had adopted children of color.

Table 1. Family Structure*

Family Structure	Number of Families	Percent
Married couples	104	65%
Unmarried couples-same sex	2	1%
Unmarried couples-opposite sex	3	2%
Single females	47	29%
Single males	5	3%
Total = 161 Families	**161**	**100%**

*Percentages are calculated on the total number of families in the sample (N = 161).

Table 2. Education Level of Adoptive Parents*

Highest Education Achieved	Mothers	Fathers
Grade school or some high school	3 (2%)	2 (2%)
High school diploma or GED	9 (6%)	13 (11%)
Some college (includes junior or community college)	42 (27%)	31 (27%)
Technical, vocational, or trade school	9 (6%)	9 (8%)
College graduate (Bachelor's degree)	50 (32%)	26 (23%)
Graduate school (Master's or Ph.D.)	40 (26%)	22 (19%)
Other	2 (1%)	3 (3%)
Missing information	1 (1%)	8 (7%)
Total = 270 Parents**	**156**	**114**

*Percentages are calculated on the total for each column (e.g., n = 156 mothers).
**Percentages do not always add to 100% due to rounding.

Table 3. Family Race/Ethnicity*

Family Race/Ethnicity	Number	Percent
Caucasian (non-Hispanic)	128	80%
African American	18	11%
Interracial	9	6%
Hispanic	5	3%
Mixed race/ethnicity	1	1%
Total**	**161**	

*Percentages are calculated on the total number of families in the sample (N = 161).
**Percentages do not always add to 100% due to rounding

Table 4. Family Race/Ethnicity by Child Race/Ethnicity*

Child's Race/ Ethnicity	Family Race/Ethnicity						
	Caucasian	**African American**	**Hispanic**	**Native American**	**Mixed Race/ Ethnicity*****	**Inter-racial******	**Total****
Caucasian	78 (48%)	0 (0%)	0 (0%)	0 (0%)	0 (0%)	2 (1%)	**80 (50%)**
African American	15 (9%)	14 (9%)	0 (0%)	0 (0%)	0 (0%)	2 (1%)	**31 (19%)**
Hispanic	12 (7%)	1 (1%)	5 (3%)	0 (0%)	0 (0%)	2 (1%)	**20 (12%)**
Native American	3 (2%)	0 (0%)	0 (0%)	0 (0%)	0 (0%)	0 (0%)	**3 (2%)**
Mixed race/ ethnicity***	20 (12%)	3 (2%)	0 (0%)	0 (0%)	1 (1%)	3 (2%)	**27 (17%)**
Total Families**	**128 (80%)**	**18 (11%)**	**5 (3%)**	**0 (0%)**	**1 (1%)**	**9 (6%)**	**161 (100%)**

*Percentages are calculated on the total number of families in the sample (N = 161).
**Percentages do not always add to 100% due to rounding.
*** Mixed race/ethnicity includes biracial and multiracial individuals. The mixed race/ethnicity family includes two parents who are both similarly mixed (African American and Caucasian, for example).
****Interracial includes couples whose racial/ethnic backgrounds are not the same.

Table 5. Number of Adopted Children*

Number of Adopted Children per Family	Number of Families	Percent
One	55	34%
Two	47	29%
Three	13	8%
Four	17	11%
Five	12	7%
Six	8	5%
Seven	3	2%
Eight	2	1%
Nine	3	2%
Ten	1	1%
Total	**161**	**100%**

*Percentages are calculated on the total number of families in the sample (N= 161).

5. Number of Adopted Children

Of the 161 families, 106 (66 percent) had adopted more than one child. Forty-seven of the multiple adopters (29 percent) had adopted two children (including the focus child), and 42 (26 percent) had adopted between three and five children. Seventeen families (11 percent) had adopted between six and 10 children.

6. Ages of Children in the Home

Almost all of the families in this study (97 percent) were parenting children who were school age or older. Two-thirds of the sample (n = 107, 66 percent) were parenting at least one teenager at the time of the study. Four families (two percent) were parenting only children less than five years of age.

7. Type of Adoption by Family Status

Of the 161 families who participated in the Success Factors study, 94 (58 percent) were general adopters (not adopting a specific child they were fostering or knew before placement). Of the remaining families, 41 (25 percent) had adopted a child they had fostered, six (four percent) adopted a relative, and 20 (12 percent) adopted a specific child but not one they had fostered. In this latter group, families had initially come into contact with these children due to the parents' roles as their therapist, teacher, residential treatment worker, or through family friends who were fostering the children. After meeting and interacting with the children, the families decided they wanted to adopt them.

8. Foster Parent Adopters

Of the 161 families, 32 adoptive families (20 percent) were also fostering children in their home. The majority of these 32 families (n = 26, 81 percent) had one or two foster children living in the home in addition to their adopted child[ren]. The remaining 129 families (80 percent) were not currently fostering any children.

9. Type of Adoption Agency

Public agencies facilitated the adoptions for 93 families (58 percent), and private agencies facilitated placements for 68 families (42 percent).

Table 6. Ages of Children in the Home*

Children's Ages	Number	Percent
School age and teens (5-2 1 yrs.)	45	28%
Teens only (13-21 yrs.)	37	23%
School age only (5-12 yrs.)	32	20%
Preschool, school age and teens (0-2 1 yrs.)	25	16%
Preschool and school age (0-12 yrs.)	16	10%
Preschool only (< 5 yrs.)	4	2%
Missing information	2	1%
Total	**161**	**100%**

*Percentages are calculated on the total number of families in the sample (N = 161).

Table 7. Type of Adoption*

General Adopters	Foster Parent Adopters	Relative Adopters	Specific Child Adopters (non Foster Child)	Total Families**
94 (58%)	41 (25%)	6 (4%)	20 (12%)	**161**

*Percentages are calculated on the total number of families in the sample (N = 161).
**Percentages do not always add to 100% due to rounding.

Table 8. Number of Adoptive Families Currently Fostering Children*

Number of Children Currently Being Fostered	Number of Adoptive Families	Percent
Zero	129	80%
One	16	10%
Two	10	6%
Three	4	2%
Four	1	1%
Five	1	1%
Total	**161**	**100%**

*Percentages are calculated on the total number of families in the sample (N = 161).

Table 9. Type of Adoption Agency*

Agency Type	Number	Percent
Private	68	42%
Public	93	58%
Total	**161**	**100%**

*Percentages are calculated on the total number of families in the sample (N = 161).

C. Demographic Characteristics of Focus Children

1. Age at Placement and Time in Adoptive Home

Focus children were an average of six and a half years of age (range = 0 to 17 years) at the time of placement in the adoptive home. One hundred nineteen focus children (74 percent) in the study were between five and 17 at time of placement. Of this number, six (four percent) were between 13 and 17; 39 (24 percent) were between nine and 12; and 74 (46 percent) were between five and eight at placement. Typically, focus children had been in the home an average of six years at the time of the interview (range = one to 14 years). The remaining 42 children (26 percent) were four years old or younger. The average length of time between the time of finalization of the adoption and the time of the interview was 3.5 years.

2. Race/Ethnicity of Focus Child

Of the 161 children who were the focus of the study, 80 (50 percent) were Caucasian (non-Hispanic) and the other half were children of color. Specifically, 31 children (19 percent) were African American, 20 (12 percent) were Hispanic, three (two percent) were Native American, and 27 (17 percent) were of mixed race/ethnicity.

3. Gender of Focus Child

Of the 161 focus children, 89 (55 percent) were male and 72 (45 percent) were female.

Table 10. Age of Focus Child at Time of Placement*

Age at Placement	Number	Percent
0 – 1	21	13%
2 – 4	21	13%
5 – 8	74	46%
9 – 12	39	24%
13 – 17	6	4%
Total	**161**	**100%**

*Percentages are calculated on the total number of families in the sample (N = 161).

Table 11. Race/Ethnicity of Focus Child*

Race/Ethnicity	Number of Families	Percent
Caucasian (non-Hispanic)	80	50%
African American	31	19%
Hispanic	20	12%
Native American	3	2%
Mixed race/ethnicity	27	17%
Total	**161**	**100%**

*Percentages are calculated on the total number of families in the sample (N = 161).

Table 12. Gender of Focus Child*

Gender	Number	Percent
Males	89	55%
Females	72	45%
Total	**161**	**100%**

*Percentages are calculated on the total number of families in the sample (N = 161).

VI. Study 2

Success Factors Study: Family Factors Associated with Successful Adoptive Families

A. Adoptive Family Structure

1. Number of Children Adopted by Family Structure

This section provides data related to the first research question: were there significant differences between the types of children adopted by single adopters and couples.

One hundred sixty-one families (270 individual adoptive parents) participated in the study. One hundred nine families (68 percent) were two-parent families, 47 families (29 percent) were headed by single females, and five families (three percent) were headed by single males.

Thirty-four percent of the families had adopted only one child; 29 percent had adopted one sibling group; and 37 percent of the families had adopted more than one unrelated child, including multiple sibling groups. Over time, these multiple adopters had adopted single children, single children and sibling groups, or multiple sibling groups. Couples and single females were almost equally likely to adopt more than one unrelated child, while no single males did so.

2. Current Household Composition

Couples had a significantly larger number of biological children still in the home and a greater number of foster children than single adopters had. However, there were no statistically significant differences in the number of children adopted by family type.

3. Type of Child Adopted by Family Structure

While the data show that single women had adopted a slightly higher mean number of boys (1.57) than girls (1.26) and a greater percentage (23 percent) had adopted older children than couples (17 percent), the differences were not statistically significant. Nor was the extent to which couples and singles adopted sibling groups significantly different. There was, however, a statistically significant difference in the number of Caucasian single women who had transracially adopted (58 percent) compared to the percentage of Caucasian couples who had transracially adopted (30 percent). Caucasian single women were significantly more likely than couples to have adopted at least one child of color.

4. Families' Level of Support for Adoption

This section provides data related to the second research question: are there differences in level of support for the adoption pre- and post-placement.

Parents were asked about the level of support they received from family and friends at the time of their initial decision to adopt and after the adoption. At the initial decision to adopt, 41 percent of families had received a positive reaction from both friends and family for their decision, and 17 percent had received mixed reactions from friends and family. Thirty-seven percent of the families reported that they either had support from their families or their friends, but not both. However, overall at post-placement, parents in the study reported fairly high levels of support from family and friends. Seventy-four percent of the families reported positive support for the adoption post-placement from both families and friends. Only four percent reported mixed support post-placement. This change in level of positive reaction to their initial decision to adopt and reaction at the time of the interview was statistically significant ($p < .0\ 1$).

B. Post-Adoption Services

1. Utilization of Post-Adoption Services

This section provides data related to the third research question: what kinds of post-placement services were provided to the families and what were their needs.

Table 13. Number of Children Adopted by Family Structure*

Family Structure	Couples**	Single Females	Single Males	Overall
Adopted 1 child	32%	38%	40%	34%
Adopted 1 sibling group	29%	23%	60%	29%
Adopted more than 1 unrelated child (including multiple sibling groups)	39%	38%	0%	37%

*Percentages are calculated on the total number of families in the sample (N = 161).
**Percentages do not always add to 100% due to rounding.

Table 14. Household Composition by Family Structure

Household Composition	Couples	Single Females	Single Males	Overall
Mean number of adopted children	2.7	2.8	2.4	2.7
Mean number of biological children	1.5	1.2	0.0	1.3
Mean number of foster children	0.6	0.4	0.4	0.5
Mean number of total children in the home*	3.6	2.8	2.8	3.4

* $p < .05$; Significance level calculations do not include single males due to small sample size.

Table 15. Type of Child Adopted by Family Structure*

Type of Adopted Child	Couples**	Single Females	Single Males	Total
Mean number of adopted girls	1.32	1.26	0.60	1.28
Mean number of adopted boys	1.34	1.57	1.80	1.42
% adopted at least 1 sibling group	53%	51%	20%	53%
% adopted at least 1 child 11 and older	17%	23%	0%	19%
% adopted at least 1 child transraci-ally (Caucasian families only) (***)	30%	58%	75%	44.5%

*Percentages are calculated on the total number of families in the sample (N = 161).

**Percentages will not add to 100% as these items are not mutually exclusive.

*** $p < .05$; Significance level calculations do not include single males due to small sample size.

Included in the family measures was a structured checklist designed to assess which post- adoption services families used and how helpful these services were to the families. Families rated helpfulness on a 5-point scale: 1) not at all helpful, 2) not very helpful, 3) somewhat helpful, 4) very helpful, and 5) extremely helpful. Families were also asked to check which services they needed but had not received.

Families reported using an average of 13 different types of post-adoption services. They also reported that they found the majority of services (76 percent) were either very helpful or extremely helpful. In addition, parents reported that they needed, on average, six services that they did NOT receive.

Table 16. Families' Level of Support for Adoption*

Level of Support	Initial Decision to Adopt		Post-placement	
	n	%	n	%
Positive support from both relatives and friends	66	41%	119	74%
Positive support from relatives or friends, but not both	60	37%	34	21%
Mixed support	27	17%	6	4%
Unsupportive relatives and friends	4	2%	1	1%
Missing information	4	2%	1	1%
Total**	**161**		**161**	

*Percentages are calculated on the total number of families in the sample (N = 161).
**Percentages do not always add to 100% due to rounding.

2. Post-Adoption Services Received

The most commonly reported post-adoption services identified by families in this study were financial supports, including adoption subsidies (89 percent), and help with routine medical (79 percent) and dental (77 percent) care. Seventy-seven percent also reported receiving financial supports other than a subsidy, such as health insurance, medical subsidies, and social security benefits. The next most common set of services families used addressed the child's psychological and educational needs. Seventy-one percent of families reported using individual child therapy post-adoption; 60 percent had educational assessments completed; and 59 percent of the children had psychological evaluations.

In addition to utilizing post-adoption services for their children, many families also identified supports for themselves. For example, 56 percent of families reported spending time with other adoptive parents as a support mechanism, and 47 percent reported using family therapy. Only three percent of the families indicated they did not use any post-adoption services.

3. Most Helpful Post-Adoption Services

Over 75 percent of the families received an adoption subsidy or help with routine medical and dental care. Ninety percent or more of the families who received these three services found them very or extremely helpful. Other services were found to be helpful, but not as helpful as the subsidy or medical/dental care. For example, 63 to 79 percent of families found various types of counseling, trainings, and support groups helpful. Between 69 and 76 percent of the families who received counseling on parenting skills, abuse, separation, sexual, and adoption issues found the service to be very or extremely helpful.

Table 17. Post-Adoption Services Received*

Type of Service	Number of Families Receiving this Service	Percentage of Families Receiving this Service **
Adoption subsidy	130	89%
Routine medical care	116	79%
Dental care	113	77%
Other financial supports	112	77%
Individual child therapy	104	71%
Educational assessment	87	60%
Psychological evaluation	86	59%
Time with other adoptive parents	82	56%
Special education curriculum	76	52%
Family therapy	68	47%
Time with other adopted children	58	40%
Time with experienced adoptive parents	57	39%
Adoptive parent support group	56	38%
Parenting skills counseling	56	38%
Adoption issues counseling	56	38%
Abuse issues counseling	56	38%
Separation issues counseling	52	36%
Respite care (overnight)	46	32%
Speech therapy	43	29%
Legal services[19]	41	28%
Social work service coordination	38	26%
Child development counseling	36	25%
Sexual issues counseling	35	24%
Daycare: out-of-home	32	22%
Daycare: in-home	32	22%
Physical or occupational therapy	30	21%

Type of Service	Number of Families Receiving this Service	Percentage of Families Receiving this Service **
Child's future counseling	28	19%
Tutoring	27	18%
Support group for adopted child	26	18%
Psychiatric hospitalization	23	16%
Medical care for disability	19	13%
Out-of-home placement (residential treatment, group home, rehabilitation facility, etc.)	19	13%
Counseling to prevent outside placement	17	12%
Daycare for child w/psychiatric problems	13	9%
Transracial counseling	13	9%
Daycare for a disabled child	10	7%
Emergency shelter care[20]	7	5%
Home health nurse	6	4%
Homemaker/housekeeper	5	3%
Drug/alcohol services	3	2%

*Percentages are calculated on the total number of families who responded to the survey (n = 146 of the original 161 families).

** Percentages do not add up to 100% as parents could report using multiple services.

About 67 percent of the families found their child's individual therapy to be very or extremely helpful. Two-thirds or more of families found that 10 out of 11 types of counseling were very or extremely helpful, while 50 percent of families found counseling to prevent an outof-home placement to be very or extremely helpful.

Seventy-three percent of the parents who spent time with other adoptive parents found the activity very or extremely helpful, and 51 percent of the families whose children spent time with other adopted children found the activity very helpful. Although fewer parents (18 percent) reported that their children were in a formal adoption support group, 63 percent found the group to be very helpful for their children.

Table 18. Helpfulness of Services Received*

Type of Service	Number of Families Receiving Services	Percentage Finding Service Very or Extremely Helpful**	Missing Values**
Medical care for disability	19	100%	0%
Daycare: out-of-home	32	97%	3%
Legal services	41	95%	2%
Adoption subsidy	130	93%	2%
Routine medical care	116	91%	2%
Transracial adoption counseling***	13	91%	15%
Dental care	113	91%	4%
Daycare: in-home	32	90%	3%
Other financial supports	112	87%	1%
Speech therapy	43	84%	0%
Respite care (overnight)	46	83%	0%
Tutoring	27	81%	0%
Homemaker/housekeeper	5	80%	0%
Child development counseling***	36	79%	6%
Physical or occupational therapy	30	79%	3%
Special education classes	76	79%	0%
Family therapy***	68	77%	3%
Daycare for child w/psychiatric problems	13	77%	0%
Abuse issues counseling***	56	76%	4%
Adoption issues counseling***	56	75%	2%
Separation issues counseling***	52	75%	2%
Time with experienced adoptive parents	57	73%	2%
Time with other adoptive parents	82	73%	2%
Emergency shelter care	7	71%	0%
Educational assessment	87	71%	2%
Adoptive parent support group	56	70%	4%
Parenting skills counseling***	56	70%	4%

Type of Service	Number of Families Receiving Services	Percentage Finding Service Very or Extremely Helpful**	Missing Values**
Psychological evaluation	86	70%	5%
Social work service coordination	38	69%	5%
Sexual issues counseling***	35	69%	0%
Home health nurse	6	67%	0%
Child's future counseling***	28	67%	4%
Individual child therapy***	104	67%	5%
Out of home placement	19	67%	5%
Support group for adopted child	26	63%	8%
Daycare for a disabled child	10	60%	0%
Time with other adopted children	58	51%	2%
Counseling to prevent outside placement	17	50%	6%
Psychiatric hospitalization	23	50%	4%
Drug/alcohol services	3	0%	0%

*Percentages in the second column are calculated on the total number of families who received each service, as reported in the previous table (Table 17) (e.g., n = 19 for medical care for disability). Percentages in the third column are calculated on the number of families who received each service, but did not provide data on how helpful the service was (i.e., 15% of the 13 families who had transracial counseling did not report whether it was helpful or not).

** Percentages do not add up to 100% as these items are not mutually exclusive.

***Helpful or very helpful counseling services for 50% or more of the respondents.

4. Unmet Service Needs

The top five most needed services were accessed by over 80 percent of the parents reporting need. For example, of the 96 families who said they needed a subsidy, only four families (four percent) did not get it. Similarly, of the 104 families who said they needed dental services for the child, 15 (14 percent) were unable to get the dental services they needed.

There were, however, a number of other services that many of the families needed but were unable to access. For example, 86 families (59 percent of the sample) said they needed respite care (overnight), but 48 of those families (56 percent) were unable to get respite. Similarly, 80 families (55 percent) said they wanted counseling for adoption issues, but 39 families (49 percent) did not receive it. Equally needed but not received were a support group for the adopted child, tutoring services, in-home day care, out-of-home day care, time with experienced adoptive parents, and an adoptive parent support group. Close to half of all the families said they needed these six services, but only 50 percent or less of those families received them.

Among the services needed by a third or fewer families, the most unmet needs were for homemaker/housekeeper services (93 percent did not receive services), day care for children with psychiatric problems (70 percent did not receive services), and drug or alcohol services for children (67 percent did not receive services).

Table 19. Unmet Service Needs*

Type of Service	Number and % of Adoptive Families who Needed Specific Service**		Of the Families Needing a Specific Service, the Number and % Who Never Received It**	
	n	%	n	%
Dental care	104	71%	**15	14%
Adoption subsidy	96	66%	4	4%
Routine medical care	95	65%	6	6%
Other financial supports	88	60%	14	16%
Individual child therapy	87	60%	9	10%
	n	%	n	%
Respite care (overnight)	86	59%	48	56%
Family therapy	81	55%	27	33%
Adoption issues counseling	80	55%	39	49%
Time with other adoptive parents	79	54%	27	34%
Educational assessment	78	53%	14	18%
Time with experienced adoptive parents	75	51%	39	52%
Adoptive parent support group	75	51%	39	52%
Psychological evaluation	73	50%	9	12%
Daycare: in-home	69	47%	44	64%
Special education classes	66	45%	8	12%
Time with other adopted children	65	45%	32	49%
Support group for adopted child	64	44%	51	80%
Daycare: out-of-home	62	42%	35	56%
Parenting skills counseling	62	42%	23	37%
Tutoring	62	42%	40	65%
Separation issues counseling	61	42%	26	43%
Abuse issues counseling	58	40%	21	36%
Social work service coordination	53	36%	23	43%

Child's future counseling	50	34%	32	64%
Legal services	50	34%	18	36%
Sexual issues counseling	48	33%	23	48%
Child development counseling	41	28%	17	41%
Homemaker/housekeeper	40	27%	37	93%
Speech therapy	38	26%	7	18%
Daycare for a child with psychiatric problems	37	25%	26	70%
Physical or occupational therapy	29	20%	4	14%
Counseling to prevent outside placement	28	19%	13	46%
Transracial issues counseling	25	17%	15	60%
Psychiatric hospitalization	25	17%	4	16%
	n	**%**	**n**	**%**
Daycare for a disabled child	22	15%	13	59%
Out of home placement	22	15%	5	23%
Medical care for disability	18	12%	4	22%
Emergency shelter care	16	11%	9	56%
Drug/alcohol services	9	6%	6	67%
Home health/nursing	6	4%	2	33%

*Percentages in column 2 are calculated on the total number of parents who responded to the survey (n = 146 of the original 161 parents). Percentages in column 3 are calculated on the number of parents who needed each service, as reported in column 2 (e.g., 15 of the 104 parents who needed dental care did not receive it).

**Percentages across columns 2 and 3 will not add to 100% because column 3 is a subset of column 2. In other words, 14% (column 3) of the 71% (column 2) of families needing dental care services never received that service.

5. Concerns Parents have with Utilization of Post-Adoption Services

The most frequently named concerns with utilizing post-adoption services were lack of time and lack of confidence in service providers. Forty-one percent of families in the sample reported a problem with finding time to access services, while 40 percent reported a lack of confidence in service providers. Other concerns raised by approximately one-third of the 146 families who used post-adoption services were: insurance does not cover services (35 percent), lack of qualified providers in the area (34 percent), service providers do not understand problems (32 percent), families are unable to find the right services (32 percent), and services are not available at the right time (29 percent).

C. Child Behavior Challenges and Parental Stress

1. Adoptive Parent Stress Measured by the Parenting Stress Index

This section provides data related to the fourth research question: how significant were the children's behavioral challenges.

The level of difficulty parents had in parenting the focus child was measured in several different ways. In the interview, one parent in each of the 161 families was asked to rate how difficult the focus child has been to parent. Parents rated difficulty on a 5-point scale, with one being very easy and five being very difficult. In the survey, out of a list of 35 behaviors and attributes, parents were asked to identify the number exhibited by their child. The parents also were asked to complete four Parenting Stress Index (PSI) subscales indicating whether their child gave them positive reinforcement, whether their child was adaptable, whether their child was demanding, and whether they were accepting of their child's behavior. High scores on the PSI subscales indicate high parenting stress in the measured domains. Abidin (1995, p. 5) has normed the PSI subscales and identified cut off points for each scale. The lower cut off is at the 15th percentile or below. The higher cut off is at the 85th percentile or above. He describes families whose scores are higher than the cut off point as manifesting high levels of stress on that scale. He suggests that the families who fall below may be underreporting their levels of stress due to social desirability pressures.

Children in the study exhibited an average of 10 difficult behaviors. Only 32 parents (20 percent) described the focus child as easy or very easy to parent. Thirty-six (22 percent) described the child as somewhat easy. However, over half, 93 parents (58 percent) described their child as difficult or very difficult to parent.

On each of the four PSI subscales, the responses of more than half of the parents indicated high parenting stress. The highest percentage of parents, 69 percent, identified high parenting stress associated with the demandingness of the child (subscale).

2. Child Behavior Challenges, Parenting Difficulty, and Parental Stress

As shown in Table 22, Pearson's correlation was used to measure the association between the parents' assessment of how difficult the focus child was to parent and the more objective measure, "Total Number of Behavior Problems," and with the four normed PSI measures.[21] All of the measures were significantly, positively associated ($p < .01$) with the parent's assessment.

The PSI score "Child is Demanding" and the "Total Number of Behavior Problems" scores had the highest correlations at r = .67 and r = .68 respectively.

Table 20. Concerns with Utilization of Services*

Concern	Number of Families with this Concern	% of Families with this Concern**
Lack of time to access services	60	41%
Lack of confidence in service providers	59	40%
Insurance does not cover services	51	35%
Lack of qualified service providers in area	49	34%
Service providers do not understand problems	47	32%
Cannot find the right services	46	32%
Services are not available at the right time	42	29%
Family does not know where the services are located	35	24%
Focus child will not go for counseling	33	23%
Transportation is a problem	23	16%
The services are not culturally sensitive	22	15%
The family will not go for counseling	14	10%
Services are offered by a different religious group	10	7%

*Percentages are calculated on the total number of families who responded to the survey (n = 146 of the original 161 families).

** Percentages do not add up to 100% as parents could report multiple concerns.

Table 21. Adoptive Parent Stress Measured by the PSI*

PSI Subscale Content	High**	Normal	Low	Missing
Child does not give positive reinforcement to parent	58%	36%	5%	1%
Child is not adaptable	61%	30%	9%	0%
Child is demanding	69%	23%	8%	0%
Parent does not accept child	64%	30%	6%	0%

*Percentages are calculated on the total number of families who responded to the survey (n = 146 of the original 161 families).

** Percentages do not add up to 100% as parents could report multiple stressors.

Table 22. Child Behavior Problems, Parenting Difficulty, and Parental Stress

		Total Number of Behavioral Problems	PSI: Child Does Not Give Positive Reinforcement to Parent	PSI: Parent Does Not Accept Child	PSI: Child is Not Adaptable	PSI: Child is Demanding
Parent assessment of level of difficulty	r	0.68*	0.45*	0.51*	0.57*	0.67*
	N	146	145	146	146	146

* p < .01

3. Children's Significant Behavior Challenges

This section provides data related to the fifth research question: what were the most significant child behavior challenges.

One parent from each family was asked to report on what types of attributes the children exhibited and behaviors in which the children engaged that made the children difficult to parent. Responses were received from 146 (91 percent) of the 161 parents. The most common child attributes parents addressed were: anger (64 percent), defiance (60 percent), impulsiveness (60 percent), and manipulation (46 percent). The most common types of behaviors were: violating rules of conduct (49 percent), lying (49 percent), arguing with peers (45 percent), and tantrums (45 percent).

Table 23 shows a fairly low percentage of the children described as "easy" to parent engaging in challenging behaviors, with the exception of lying (29 percent) and tantrums (25 percent). The group labeled by the parents as difficult had a much larger percentage of children who were engaged in more serious behavior problems such as: violating rules of conduct (70 percent), verbal aggression (55 percent), physical aggression (48 percent), stealing (48 percent), and vandalism (31 percent).

In summary, children described as difficult to parent displayed behavior challenges including violating rules of conduct (70 percent), verbal (55 percent) and physical (48 percent) aggression, stealing (48 percent), and vandalism (31 percent). This group was also more likely to be defiant, manipulative and/or depressed. Children in this category also were reported to have an average of five disabilities/challenges.

Table 23. Child Attributes and Behaviors Related to Level of Parenting Difficulty*

Attributes	Easy (n = 28)**	Somewhat Easy (n = 29)	Difficult (n = 89)	Overall (n = 146)
Anger	14%	66%	79%	64%
Defiance	18%	48%	78%	60%
Impulsive	14%	48%	78%	60%
Manipulative	25%	24%	60%	46%
Disobedient	0%	17%	61%	40%
Hyperactivity	7%	38%	49%	39%
Irritability	0%	3%	39%	25%
Depression	11%	14%	40%	29%
Inability to attach to family members	4%	10%	35%	24%
Rejects affection	4%	10%	25%	18%
Cruelty	0%	0%	13%	8%
Withdrawn	14%	3%	12%	11%
Behaviors				
Violating rules of conduct	14%	21%	70%	49%
Lying	29%	34%	61%	49%
Argues with peers	14%	31%	58%	45%
Tantrums	25%	31%	56%	45%
Argues with siblings	11%	31%	56%	42%
Verbal aggression	0%	14%	55%	36%
Physical aggression	4%	14%	48%	33%
Stealing	18%	21%	48%	37%
Sabotaging relationships	4%	10%	43%	29%
Vandalism	0%	3%	31%	20%
Running away	0%	0%	27%	16%
Self abuse	0%	7%	26%	17%
Sexual acting out	7%	14%	25%	19%

*Percentages are calculated on the total number in each column (e.g., n = 28 parents who reported their child as "easy" to parent).

** Percentages do not add up to 100% as parents could report multiple child attributes.

4. Children's Disabilities and Other Special Needs

Over half of the sample of adopted children had some type of attention deficit diagnosis (55 percent) and half had learning disabilities (50 percent). The two most commonly mentioned child challenges were behavioral problems and emotional problems. Over three-quarters of the children were characterized by the adoptive parents as having behavioral problems, while 68 percent of the children were characterized as having emotional problems.

D. Parental Satisfaction with Parenting, their Marriage, and their Child's Adoption

1. Parental Satisfaction Measures and Scores

This section provides data related to the sixth research question: how satisfied are parents with their parenting, their marriage, and their child's adoption.

One parent from each family was asked to complete several measures of satisfaction that were used in this study. Satisfaction with parenting in general[22] was measured using a 10-item scale from Reilly and Platz (2003). Marital satisfaction was assessed using a 5-item scale adapted from Fowers and Olson (1993). Parents' individual item scores were totaled, then averaged, in order to get marital satisfaction scores; scores fell between one and five, with five indicating the highest level of satisfaction. For parenting satisfaction scores, scores fell between one and four, with four indicating the highest level of satisfaction. Parents were also asked to rate on a scale of one to five, with five indicating very satisfied, how satisfied they were with the adoption of the focus child. Parents in the study reported being very satisfied with the adoption of the focus child (4.6 on a 5-point scale) and very satisfied with parenting in general (3.5 on a 4- point scale). For those who were married, parents were satisfied with their marital relationship (4.2 on a 5-point scale).

2. Relationship between Parenting and Marital Satisfaction

Pearson's correlation was also used to examine the association between marital satisfaction, satisfaction with parenting in general, and satisfaction with the focus child's adoption.[23] Satisfaction with parenting in general was significantly, albeit modestly, correlated with satisfaction with the adoption of the focus child ($r = .26$) as well as marital satisfaction ($r = .24$). However, a statistically significant relationship was not found between marital satisfaction and satisfaction with the adoption of the focus child.

E. Adoptive Family Contact with Birthparents

This section provides data related to the seventh research question: are there differences in characteristics of families who have contact with the birthparents and those who do not have contact with any foster or birth family members from the child's past.

Table 24. Children's Disabilities and Other Special Needs*

Child Disabilities & Other Special Needs	n	%**
Behavioral problems	111	76%
Emotional problems	100	68%
ADD or ADHD	81	55%
Learning disability	73	50%
Psychiatric problems	70	48%
Developmental delays	51	35%
Chronic medical, non-life threatening	26	18%
Mental retardation or handicap	21	14%
Motor disability	11	8%
Serious speech impairment or muteness	8	5%
Physical handicap (orthopedic)	7	5%
Serious vision impairment or blindness	7	5%
Autism	6	4%
Seizure disorder	6	4%
Serious hearing impairment or deafness	4	3%
Physical handicap (non-orthopedic)	4	3%
Cerebral Palsy	3	2%
Chronic medical, terminal	3	2%

*Percentages are calculated on the total number of families who responded to the survey (n = 146 of the original 161 families).

** Percentages do not add up to 100% as parents could report multiple disabilities /challenges.

Table 25. Parental Satisfaction with their Marriage, the Child's Adoption, and Parenting

Satisfaction	Mean	Number of Parents*
Marital satisfaction	4.2 (of a possible 5)	94
Focus child's adoption	4.6 (of a possible 5)	161
Parenting in general	3.5 (of a possible 4)	141

*The number of parents varies on this table due to using married parents for one analysis and due to missing data.

Table 26. Relationship between Parenting and Marital Satisfaction

Satisfaction	Pearson's Correlation	Parenting in General	Focus Child's Adoption
Marital satisfaction	r	0.24*	0.15
	n	90	94
Parenting in general	r	—	0.26**
	n	—	141

* p < .05
** p < .01

Table 27. Family Structure*

Family Structure	Number	Percent
Married couples	19	66%
Single females	10	34%
Total	**29**	**100%**

*Percentages are calculated on the total number of families in this sample (n = 29).

In the interview, the adoptive families (N = 161) were asked whether they have had post- placement contact with anyone from the child's past and to give reasons for the presence or absence of such contact. In addition, families who had post-placement contact were asked to describe the type and frequency of contact and whether the contact continued post-finalization. Coders gathered information from the interviews concerning contact with: birth-parents; siblings; extended birth relatives; foster families; professional staff; and other important individuals such as teachers, neighbors, or friends. For the purposes of this chapter, two types of contact were compared—those families who have had post-placement contact with birthparents and those families who have had no post-placement contact with birth or foster families.

1. Demographic Characteristics of Families who had Post-Finalization Contact with Birthparents

a. Family Structure

Twenty-nine adoptive families (18 percent) in the sample had post-finalization contact with at least one birthparent. Although the majority of the adoptive families (n = 19, 66 percent) with contact were married couples, there were also 10 (34 percent) single female adopters.

b. Age, Family Income, and Education

At the time of data collection, the average age of the adoptive mothers was 46 years and adoptive fathers was 47 years. The adoptive families had an average income of $52,060. The average income for couples was $68,314 and $32,042 for the single, female adopters. More than half of the sample of adoptive mothers had completed either a bachelor's or a graduate degree, whereas more than half of the sample of adoptive fathers had not completed college. Below is a detailed description of the parents' educational levels.

Table 28. Education Level of Adoptive Parents*

Highest Education Achieved	Mothers	Fathers
Grade school or some high school	1 (3%)	0 (0%)
High school diploma or GED	1 (3%)	5 (26%)
Some college (includes junior or community college)	6 (2 1%)	5 (26%)
Technical, vocational, or trade school	2 (7%)	1 (5%)
Highest Education Achieved	**Mothers**	**Fathers**
College graduate (Bachelor's degree)	11 (38%)	1 (5%)
Graduate school (Master's or Ph.D.)	8 (28%)	5 (26%)
Other	0 (0%)	0 (0%)
Missing information	0 (0%)	2 (11%)
Total = 48 adoptive parents**	**29**	**19**

*Percentages are calculated on the total for each column (n = 29 mothers).

** Percentages do not add up to 100% due to rounding.

Table 29. Race/Ethnicity of Families*

Family Race/Ethnicity	Number	Percent
Caucasian (non-Hispanic)	21	72%
African American	4	14%
Interracial	3	10%
Hispanic	0	0%
Mixed race/ethnicity	1	3%
Total**	**29**	

**Percentages are calculated on the total number of families in this sample (n = 29).

** Percentages do not add up to 100% due to rounding.

c. Family Race/Ethnicity

The majority of families (n = 21, 72 percent) identified their racial/ethnic background as Caucasian and (n = 4, 14 percent) reported their ethnic background as African American. In this sample, there were three interracial couples (10 percent) including Caucasian and African American, African American and Hispanic, Hispanic and Native American, and one couple (three percent) was of mixed race/ethnicity (e.g., both participants were Caucasian and African American).

d. Transracial and Same-race Adoptive Families: Family and Focus Child Race/Ethnicity

Overall, the majority (n = 21, 72 percent) of the 29 families adopted children of the same ethnic background as one or both parents. However, eight families (28 percent) transracially adopted. Of the transracial adopters, the majority were Caucasian families who adopted children of color.

Table 30. Family Race/Ethnicity by Child Race/Ethnicity*

Child's Race/Ethnicity	Race/Ethnicity of Adoptive Family						
	Caucasian	African American	Hispanic	Native American	Mixed Race/ Ethnicity***	Interracial****	Total
Caucasian	16 (55%)	0 (0%)	0 (0%)	0 (0%)	0 (0%)	1 (3%)	**17 (59%)**
African American	0 (0%)	4 (14%)	0 (0%)	0 (0%)	0 (0%)	2 (7%)	**6 (21%)**
Hispanic	0 (0%)	0 (0%)	0 (0%)	0 (0%)	0 (0%)	0 (0%)	**0 (0%)**
Native American	1 (3%)	0 (0%)	0 (0%)	0 (0%)	0 (0%)	0 (0%)	**1 (3%)**
Mixed race/ ethnicity***	4 (14%)	0 (0%)	0 (0%)	0 (0%)	1 (3%)	0 (0%)	**5 (17%)**
Total**	**21 (72%)**	**4 (14%)**	**0 (0%)**	**0 (0%)**	**1 (3%)**	**3 (10%)**	**29 (100%)**

*Percentages are calculated on the total number of families in this sample (n = 29).

**Percentages do not always add to 100% due to rounding.

*** Mixed race/ethnicity includes biracial and multiracial individuals. The mixed race/ethnicity family includes two parents who are both similarly mixed (African American and Caucasian, for example).

****Interracial includes couples whose racial/ethnic backgrounds are not the same.

e. Number of Adopted Children

Of the 29 families who had contact with at least one birthparent post-finalization, 20 (69 percent) had adopted more than one child. Nine of the multiple adopter families (45 percent) had adopted two children (including the focus child), and five families (25 percent) had adopted between three and five children. However, six families (30 percent) had adopted six to seven children.

j. Type of Adoption by Family Status

Of the 29 families who had post-finalization contact with at least one of the birthparents, 11 families (38 percent) had adopted a child they had fostered, and 10 families (34 percent) were general adopters (not adopting a specific child they were fostering or knew before placement). Of the remaining families, four (14 percent) adopted a relative, and four (14 percent) adopted a specific child, but one who had not been placed previously in their home. In this latter group, families initially met these children due to the parents' roles as their therapist, teacher, residential treatment worker, or through family friends who were fostering the children. The families decided they wanted to adopt the children after meeting and interacting with them.

Table 31. Number of Children Adopted*

Number of Adopted Children	Number of Families	Percent
One	9	31%
Two	9	31%
Three	2	7%
Four	2	7%
Five	1	3%
Six	5	17%
Seven	1	3%
Total**	**29**	

*Percentages are calculated on the total number of families in this sample (n = 29).
**Percentages do not always add to 100% due to rounding.

Table 32. Type of Adoption*

General Adopters	Foster Parent Adopters	Relative Adopters	Specific Child Adopters (non Foster Child)	Total Families
10 (34%)	11 (38%)	4 (14%)	4 (14%)	**29 (100%)**

*Percentages are calculated on the total number of families in this sample (n = 29).

2. Demographic Characteristics of Focus Children in Contact with Birthparents Post- Finalization

a. Age at Placement

Children from families who had post-finalization contact with birthparents were an average of 7.6 years of age at time of placement (range = 0 to 17 years) in the adoptive home. Twenty-two children (76 percent) who had contact with their birthparents post-finalization were between five and 17 at placement. Of these children, four (14 percent) were between 13 and 17 when placed, nine (31 percent) were between nine and 12 at placement, and nine (31 percent) were between five and eight at placement. The other seven children (24 percent) were age four or younger. The average length of time between placement and the time of the interview was 5.8 years and between finalization and the time of the interview was 3.5 years.

Race/Ethnicity of Focus Child

Seventeen of the 29 families (59 percent) who had contact with the children's birthparents post-finalization had focus children who were identified as Caucasian (non- Hispanic) and 12 (41 percent) were identified as children of color. Six children (21 percent) were identified as African American, one (three percent) was Native American, and five (17 percent) were mixed race/ethnicity.

Gender of Focus Child

Of the 29 focus children whose families had contact with at least one birthparent post- finalization, 18 (62 percent) were male and 11 (38 percent) were female.

Table 33. Age of Focus Child at Time of Placement*

Age at Placement	Number	Percent
0 – 1	4	14%
2 – 4	3	10%
5 – 8	9	31%
9 – 12	9	31%
13 – 17	4	14%
Total	**29**	**100%**

*Percentages are calculated on the total number of families in this sample (n = 29).

Table 34. Race/Ethnicity of Focus Child*

Race/Ethnicity	Number	Percent
Caucasian (non-Hispanic)	17	59%
African American	6	21%
Hispanic/Latino	0	0%
Native American	1	3%
Mixed race/ethnicity	5	17%
Total	**29**	**100%**

*Percentages are calculated on the total number of families in this sample (n = 29).

Table 35. Gender of Focus Child

Gender	Number	Percent
Males	18	62%
Females	11	38%
Total	**29**	**100%**

*Percentages are calculated on the total number of families in this sample (n = 29).

3. Experiences with Contact in Adoption

a. Types of Contact with Birthparents

Of the 161 families in the study, 27 families (17 percent) had no pre- or post-finalization contact with any birth or foster family members, and 48 families (30 percent) had contact with one or both of the child's birthparents either pre- or post-finalization. Of these 48 families, 19 had contact pre-finalization only, while 29 had contact post-finalization (including those who had contact both pre- and post-finalization). This chapter includes findings from an analysis of those 48 with birthparent contact and the 27 without contact with birth family or foster family members. [24]

In general, families who had contact (either pre- or post-finalization) with the child's birthparents (n = 48) were more likely to have adopted a foster child already placed in their home, or a child with whom they had a previous relationship (child-specific or relative adoption), than the 27 families who had no contact with the child's birthparents or foster family members. Families who had pre-finalization only contact with one or both birthparents (n = 19) were more likely to have court-mandated visits with birthparents than parents who had contact post- finalization. Families who had pre-finalization only contact generally had more frequent pre- finalization contact (21 percent) than the families who had contact with the child's birthparents post-finalization (14 percent). Families with pre-finalization only contact were more likely to have supervised visits with the birthparents (58 percent with birthmothers and 26 percent with birthfathers), whereas families who had post-finalization contact had a variety of types of contact, including cards, letters, and emails (31 percent with birthmothers and three percent with birthfathers); phone calls (31 percent with birthmothers and 10 percent with birthfathers); and supervised or unsupervised visits (44 percent with birthmothers and 14 percent with birthfathers).

An analysis of the reasons the adoptive parents liked or supported contact with the birthparents reveals a similar trend regarding contact with the birthmother and the birthfather. Many adoptive parents reported that they did not like anything about the contact with birthmother (n = 12, 27 percent) or birthfather (n = 7, 35 percent).[25] Over half (53 percent) of these families had pre-finalization contact only. However, a large portion of adoptive parents said they supported the contact because they respected the child's birth heritage and understood the importance of the contact with the birthmother (n = 26, 58 percent) and birthfather (n = 60, 30 percent) to the child. Adoptive parents also supported contact because the child wanted contact with birthmothers (n = five, 11 percent) and birthfathers (n = one, five percent); the adoptive parent felt empathy for the child's birthmother (n = four, nine percent); the birthmother supported the child's adoption (n = two, four percent); and because it was the child's right to have contact with birthmother (n = one, two percent).

b. Families with No Contact with Birthparents or Foster Parents

The 27 parents whose families had no contact with any birthparents or foster parents were asked why there was no contact with the child's birthparents. The most frequent reason given was that the adoptive parents never considered contact because the birthparents had their rights terminated and/or were the child's abuser [n = 16 (59 percent) for birthmothers; n = nine (33 percent) for birthfathers]. The second most common reason was that the child never knew the birthparent [n = six (22 percent) for birthmothers; n = 11 (41 percent) for birthfathers]. Other answers included: birthparent is/was in prison [n = one (four percent) for birthmothers; n = five (19 percent) for birthfathers]; concerns for the child's safety [n = three (11 percent) for birthmothers; n = four (15 percent) for birthfathers]; and the parent is troubled [n = four (15 percent) for birthmothers].[26]

c. Variations in Contact Types

Families were asked to identify what types of contact that they were participating in pre- and post-finalization and with which birthparent they were in contact. The types of contact were letters, phone calls, day visits, and overnight visits. Comparisons were made between families who had contact with one or both birthparents during the pre-finalization time only and those who had contact pre- and post-finalization or post-finalization only.

Table 36. Types of Contact with Birthparents*

	No Contact with Birthparents or Foster Families (n = 27)		Contact with Birthparents (n = 48)			
			Pre-finalization Only Contact with Birthparents (n = 19)		Post-finalization Contact with Birthparents (n = 29)	
Type of Adoption						
General adoption	16	(59%)	9	(47%)	10	(34%)
Foster child, child-specific, or relative adoption	11	(41%)	10	(53%)	19	(66%)
Mandated Contact						
Mandated visits with birthparents while child was in foster care	0	(0%)	14	(74%)	6	(21%)
Frequency of Contact Pre- Finalization**						
More frequent contact with birthmother pre-finalization	0	(0%)	4	(21%)	4	(14%)
More frequent contact with birthfather pre-finalization	0	(0%)	2	(11%)	1	(3%)
Type of Contact with Birthmother***						
Cards/letters/emails	0	(0%)	1	(5%)	9	(31%)
Phone calls	0	(0%)	1	(5%)	9	(3 1%)
Supervised visits	0	(0%)	11	(58%)	10	(34%)
Unsupervised visits	0	(0%)	1	(5%)	3	(10%)
Type of Contact with Birthfather***						
Cards/letters/emails	0	(0%)	0	(0%)	1	(3%)
Phone calls	0	(0%)	1	(5%)	3	(10%)
Supervised visits	0	(0%)	5	(26%)	4	(14%)
Unsupervised visits	0	(0%)	1	(5%)	0	(0%)

*Percentages are calculated on the total for each column (e.g., n = 27 families who had no contact with birthparents or foster families).

**Percentages may not add to 100% under "Frequency of Contact" because only those families with more frequent contact pre-finalization are reported here.

*** Percentages may not add to 100% under "Type of Contact" because families could have reported multiple types of contact with each birthparent.

Table 37. Reasons for No Contact with Birthparents*

Reasons for No Contact	Birthmother (n = 27)**	%	Birthfather (n = 27)	%
Adoptive parent never considered contact/ parental rights were terminated or was abuser	16	59%	9	33%
Child never knew the person	6	22%	11	41%
Person was or is in prison	1	4%	5	19%
Concerns for the child's safety	3	11%	4	15%
Person is troubled	4	15%	0	0%
Person is deceased	1	4%	3	11%
Divided loyalties/contact will interfere with bonding	1	4%	1	4%
Bad influence on child	0	0%	1	4%
Child does not want contact	1	4%	1	4%

*Percentages are calculated on the total for each column (e.g., n = 27 birthmothers).

**Percentages do not add to 100% because parents could have reported multiple reasons for why they have no contact with each birthparent.

There were statistically significant relationships ($p < .05$) when the following types of contact were analyzed: birthmother letters, birthmother phone calls, and birthmother day visits. More families who had contact with birthmothers through sending letters participated in this contact post-finalization only or pre- and post-finalization (39 percent); only five percent of families had this type of contact pre-finalization only. Of families who reported birthmother phone contact, five percent had pre-finalization contact only and 39 percent had post-finalization only or pre- and post-finalization contact. Sixteen percent of families with pre-finalization contact only reported birthmother day visits while 48 percent of families with post-finalization only or pre- and post-finalization contact reported birthmother day visits. There were no statistically significant relationships when analyzing any birthfather contact.

There was a statistically significant relationship for families who were mandated to have contact pre-finalization and whether they had contact post-finalization ($p < .05$). For families who were mandated to have contact with one or both birthparents pre-finalization (n = 20), the majority did not continue the contact after finalization. Of the 20 families, 70 percent had contact pre-finalization only and 30 percent reported contact post-finalization. For the 28 families who were not mandated to have contact with birthparents pre-finalization, 82 percent of them had post-finalization contact with birthparents.[27]

d. Contact and Race/Ethnicity of Adoptive Parents

When comparing families with no contact to families who had some type of contact with birthparents, there were no statistically significant differences between minority/interracial adoptive families and Caucasian adoptive families. Also, there were no statistically significant differences when comparing pre-finalization contact only with one or both birthparents and pre- and post-finalization or post-finalization only contact. Among Caucasian adoptive families, 35 percent had no contact and 65 percent had some type of contact. Of the 65 percent with some type of contact, 43 percent had pre-finalization only contact, and 57 percent had pre- and post- finalization or post-finalization only contact. Among minority/interracial adoptive families, 37 percent had no contact and 63 percent had some type of contact. Of the 63 percent with some type of contact, 33 percent had pre-finalization only contact and 67 percent had pre- and post- finalization or post-finalization only contact.

There were no statistically significant differences between families who adopted transracially and those who did not when comparing no contact with one or both birthparents and contact (pre-finalization, post-finalization or pre- and post-finalization with one or both birthparents). There were also no statistically significant differences when comparing pre- finalization contact only with one or both birthparents and pre- and post-finalization or post-finalization only contact. Among families who adopted transracially, 50 percent had no contact and 50 percent had some type of contact. Of the 50 percent with some type of contact, 54 percent had pre-finalization only contact and 46 percent had pre- and post-finalization or post- finalization only contact. Among families who did not adopt transracially, 29 percent had no contact and 71 percent had some type of contact. Of the 71 percent with some type of contact, 34 percent had pre-finalization only contact and 66 percent had pre- and post-finalization or post- finalization only contact.

e. Contact and Adoptive Parents' Education and Age

There were no statistically significant differences between levels of education of adoptive mother or adoptive fathers when comparing no contact and contact (pre-finalization, post- finalization or pre- and post-finalization with one or both birthparents). There also were no statistically significant differences when comparing pre-finalization contact only with one or both birthparents and pre- and post-finalization or post-finalization only contact. There were no statistically significant differences in level of contact when looking at adoptive parents' age.

f. Contact and Adoptive Parents' Income

There were no statistically significant differences between family income of adoptive parents when comparing no contact (mean family income $56,893) and contact (pre-finalization, post-finalization or pre- and post-finalization with one or both birthparents) (mean family income $54,444). There were also no statistically significant differences when comparing pre- finalization contact only with one or both birthparents (mean family income $57,425) and pre- and post-finalization or post-finalization only contact (mean family income $52,060).

g. Contact and Adoptive Parents' Satisfaction with Adoption

There were no statistically significant differences in the level of contact when looking at the level of satisfaction the adoptive parents felt about the adoption.

h. Contact and Age of Adopted Child

There were statistically significant differences ($p < .05$) in the level of contact when comparing the age at placement of the adopted child. For children whose families had no contact, the average age at placement was 4.69 years of age. For children whose families had some type of contact with birthparents, the average age at placement was 6.74 years.

i. Contact and Child's History

Families who adopted children who had experienced physical neglect in this sample were significantly more likely to have contact with one or both birthparents (75.6 percent) versus no contact (24.4 percent), regardless of whether physical neglect was the sole cause of the child's removal from the birth family or occurred in combination with other circumstances. There was no difference in this group when comparing pre-finalization contact only and pre- and post- finalization or post-finalization only contact.

There was a statistically significant difference ($p < .05$) in likelihood of contact if children had experienced medical neglect. In this sample, children who had experienced medical neglect were more likely to have had pre-finalization contact only (66.7 percent) than pre- and post-finalization or post-finalization only contact (33.3 percent) (regardless of whether medical neglect was the sole cause of the child's removal from the birth family or occurred in combination with other circumstances). There were no statistically significant differences when comparing contact to no contact.

There were no statistically significant differences in levels of contact when comparing the following child history factors: physical abuse, sexual abuse, emotional abuse, drug exposure, parent incarceration, parents' drug abuse, abandonment, educational neglect, domestic violence, parents' mental illness, parents' homelessness, sibling death, parents' terminal illness, or child left with relatives. Each of these circumstances could have been the sole cause of the child's removal from the birth family or could have occurred in combination with other circumstances.

j. Contact and Type of Adoption

There were statistically significant differences in the level of contact when looking at the type of adoption for child specific adopters (20 percent no contact, 80 percent some contact); foster parent adopters (33 percent no contact, 67 percent some contact); and relative or kin adopters (0 percent no contact, 100 percent some contact). Half of general adopters had contact and half did not.

F. Successful Adoptions

1. Adoptive Parents' Definition of Successful Adoption

This section provides data related to the eighth research question: how do parents in the study generally define a successful adoption.

One parent from each of the 161 families was asked to provide their definition of a successful adoption of a child with special needs. The five most frequently mentioned definitions were: 1) parents are committed to the child and the child's adoption into the family, which includes unconditional love and fully integrating the child into the family (29.8 percent); 2) child is still living in the home and not behaving negatively, such as having trouble with the law, smoking, drinking, or using drugs (21.7 percent); 3) child is showing progress in the adoptive home—the child's behavior is improving, the child is happier in the home, and physical and medical issues are being resolved or controlled (16.1 percent); 4) parent and child have bonded with each other, love each other (15.5 percent); and 5) parents were prepared to adopt a child with special needs and therefore had realistic expectations of the child (the most important part of the preparation is receiving extensive background information on the child) (14.3 percent).

One parent described success in terms of parental commitment: "Raising a kid to maturity where they are self-supporting. And not giving up. And also meeting all their needs no matter what those are. Hanging in there." Another parent described unconditional love and acceptance as important for success:

> "...They come with all these diagnoses and it's kind of overwhelming at first. ... And when you get deep in the root of them in who they are, it's not so 'special needs' anymore. It's just—they're your kid. And that's who they are."

Table 38. Definition of Successful Adoption*

Definition	Number	Percent
Parental commitment to child	48	29.8%
Child is not behaving negatively	35	21.7%
Child is showing progress in the adoptive home	26	16.1%
Parent and child bonding	25	15.5%
Parents are prepared for the child's adoption & have realistic child expectations	23	14.3%
Parents are working the system for the benefit of the child	14	8.7%
Parents have the necessary skill and temperament to parent a child with special needs	10	6.2%
Agency provides necessary services/Needs of child are met	10	6.2%
Family has support systems in place	9	5.6%
Agency provides moral support	7	4.3%
Family and child are a good match	6	3.7%
Child was prepared for the adoption	2	1.2%
Agency uses best practices with the adoptive family	2	1.2%
Family has legal support in the adoption process	1	0.6%
Agencies have screened out families unsuited to parenting children with special needs	1	0.6%

*Percentages are calculated on the total number of families in the sample (N = 161).

**Percentages do not add to 100% because parents may have reported more than one response.

A third parent focused on the role of preparation as the key to success:

> "I would define it as one that the adoptive parents goes in knowing everything that is known about the situation, that there's no secrets, there's no things that are held off until later, that they're told flat out before the placement everything that they need to know. I feel like at least some understanding of issues that could possibly be involved such as disorders that the kids might have ... And I think that any time a special needs adoption happens that the people who do the adoption should at some point have had some kind of contact with children similar to the children that they're going to adopt."

2. Success Indicators in Focus Child's Adoption

This section provides data related to the ninth research question: why do families feel the adoption of the focus child has been a success.

When families were asked if the adoption of their focus child had been a success, 141 (88 percent) said yes; 17 (11 percent) said they were not sure yet/maybe; and three (two percent) said it was not a success. Parents were also asked about the reasons they felt their adoption had been successful. The largest group, 55 families (34 percent), indicated that the child's improvement was evidence that the child's adoption was a success. Thirty-seven families (23 percent) also pointed to the fact that bonding had occurred. While meeting minimal success criteria for participation in the study (parents were still committed to the child), the three families who reported that they did not feel the adoption of their child was a success were discouraged due to the child's lack of attachment, the child's challenging behaviors, and need for out-of-home placements. The following quote illustrates these concerns:

> "We continue to be a family in crisis. And while I still love my daughter, I am very dissatisfied with or unhappy with her behaviors. Some of which relate back to her biological family, and behaviors that... I feel very let down. The promised post- adoption support never materialized."

Nearly one-fourth (24 percent) of families defined success in terms of their commitment to the child. This was often described in terms of how the child was viewed as a member of the family. Some stated that the child is "part of their family" or "is treated as if they were a biological child." Thirteen percent described their success in more minimalist terms such as the child is better off than they were before, the child is still in the home, or the adoption had not dissolved yet. Seven percent of families just said they were satisfied with how things were going or mentioned some of the rewards of adopting.

Other families pointed to the good nature of the adopted child (n = eight, five percent), or they described some parent characteristics that made the adoption a success such as having effective parenting skills (n = 10, six percent), seeking resources and information (n = six, four percent), and having had good training and information (n = six, four percent). Some families (n = seven, four percent) attributed their success to good matching on the part of the agency that placed the child with them.

Table 39. Adoption Outcome*

Outcome	Number	Percent**
Child improvement	55	34%
Commitment	38	24%
Bonding/Attachment	37	23%
Minimal/Lesser evil	21	13%
Satisfied/Rewarded	12	7%
No answers given	35	22%
Defined adoption as unsuccessful	3	1%

*Percentages are calculated on the total number of families in the sample (N = 161).

**Percentages do not add to 100% because parents may have reported more than one response.

Table 40. Success Factors*

Factors	Number	Percent**
Child		
Good child/good disposition	8	5%
Factors	**Number**	**Percent****
Parent		
Effective parenting skills	10	6%
Seeking extra resources/information	6	4%
Good training/information	6	4%
Acknowledge child's history	5	3%
Agency		
Good match	7	4%

*Percentages are calculated on the total number of families in the sample (N = 161).

**Percentages do not add to 100% because parents may have reported more than one response.

3. Families' Contributions to Success

This section provides data related to the tenth research question: what has the family contributed to the success of the focus child's adoption.

One parent from each of the 161 families was asked in what ways they believed that their family had contributed to the success of the adoption. One hundred seventeen families (73 percent) reported that commitment to the child and the adoption process was their main contribution. They gave examples of commitment as follows: "sticking it out through thick and thin" (n = 58); "fully integrating the child into the family/not treating them any differently" (n = 56); "giving the child unconditional love" (n = 29); and "willingness to dedicate extensive amounts of time to the child's development" (n = nine).

Forty-eight parents (30 percent) suggested that effective parenting skills contributed to success. The parenting skills most often identified included patience (n = 14) and consistent discipline (n = 13). Other skills mentioned included: the ability to provide routines and stability (n = seven); willingness to make changes in the family system/flexibility (n = seven); working as a team (n = six); and having good communication skills (n = six).

Thirty-three parents (20 percent) reported that they contributed to the success of the adoption by taking the initiative to expand their resource repertoire either by advocating with the public agency, schools, and the mental health system to get their children the resources they needed (n = 16) or by seeking new information on effective parenting through experts and trainings (n = 13).

Other contributions included having a support network of family and friends (n = 13, eight percent) and having realistic expectations of a child's strengths and weaknesses through participation in good training (n = 12, seven percent). Data were missing for nine families (six percent).

Table 41. Families' Contributions to Success*

Contributions	Number	Percent**
Commitment	117	73%
Effective parenting skills	48	30%
Seeking extra resources/information	33	20%
A support network	13	8%
Good training/information	12	7%
Missing data	9	6%

*Percentages are calculated on the total number of families in the sample (N = 161).

**Percentages do not add to 100% because parents may have reported more than one response.

4. Focus Child's Contributions to Success

This section provides data related to the eleventh research question: what has the focus child contributed to the success of his/her adoption.

When one parent from each of the 161 families was asked to identify how the focus child had contributed to the success of the adoption, 82 parents (51 percent) felt that improvement in the child's behavior and evidence of trying hard contributed to the success. Seventy-two parents (45 percent) reported that the child accepting the family as their own and being able to bond contributed to the success. A smaller group, 27 families (17 percent), reported that the child contributed just by being a child. Twenty families (12 percent) reported the child contributed by being a great child and/or having a sweet disposition. Two families (one percent) could not think of any ways the child had contributed to the success of the adoption, and two families (one percent) said the child had not contributed to the adoption's success. There was missing data for eight families (five percent).

Table 42. Focus Child's Contributions to Success*

Contributions	Number	Percent**
Improvement/trying hard	82	51%
Bonding/initial openness to attaching	72	45%
Being a child	27	17%
Good child/good disposition	20	12%
Could not think of ways the child contributed	2	1%
Child has not contributed anything	2	1%
Missing data/question not asked	8	5%

*Percentages are calculated on the total number of families in the sample (N = 161).
**Percentages do not add to 100% because parents may have reported more than one response.

5. Adoption Agency Contributions to Success

This section provides data related to the twelfth research question: what has the agency contributed to the success of the focus child's adoption.

Sixty families (37 percent) reported that the agency contributed by providing moral support, which included emotional support to the parents, a partnership approach, a willingness to advocate for the family, and timely communication with the parents. Fifty-three families (33 percent) said that the agency contributed nothing to the success of the adoption. Thirty-six families (22 percent) reported that the agency-provided resources or services were important to the success of their adoption.

Twenty-three families (14 percent) identified receiving good training and honest and thorough information about the focus child as important to the success of their adoption. Some examples of information parents appreciated knowing up front included that the child suffered from fetal alcohol syndrome, schizophrenia, and attachment issues. Parents reported that knowing the problems up front helped them to identify the most appropriate therapist or medication right away. The services they appreciated receiving were special attachment therapies and respite care.

Twelve families (seven percent) reported that the agencies provided at least one really helpful worker or that the agency did a really thorough job. Twelve families (seven percent) mentioned the financial support provided by the agency as contributing to the success of the adoption.

G. Families' Advice to Prospective Adoptive Parents

This section provides data related to the thirteenth research question: what advice do adoptive parents give to prospective adoptive parents and agencies.

Table 43. Agency Contributions to Success*

Contributions	Number	Percent**
Moral support	60	37%
Nothing	53	33%
Resources	36	22%
Good training/Information	23	14%
Competent practices	12	7%
Financial support	12	7%

*Percentages are calculated on the total number of families in the sample (N = 161).
**Percentages do not add to 100% because parents may have reported more than one response.

Participants were asked to provide advice to prospective adoptive parents concerning the adoption process and parenting an adopted child. Families most frequently said that they should display commitment to the child and the adoption process (n = 38, 24 percent). This included willingness to devote time and attention to the child, provide the child with opportunities to become successful, and a willingness to work with the agency. Thirty-one families (19 percent) specified the following important characteristics that adoptive families must have: flexibility, tolerance, patience, unconditional love for the child, and maintaining a sense of humor. Other responses included: the importance of advocating for the child (n = 22, 14 percent); maintaining realistic expectations of the child's strengths and weaknesses (n = 19, 12 percent); being open to discussing and/or contacting the birth family, foster family or other significant individuals from the child's past (n = 15, nine percent); interacting with other foster/adoptive parents while in the adoption process to better understand the process, as well as possible child challenges (n = 13, eight percent); the importance of fostering the child they are planning to adopt to understand the child's past and develop a relationship with him/her prior to the adoption (n = 12, seven percent); and openness to learning about and seeking available resources such as support groups, subsidies and other post-adoption services (n = 12, seven percent).

H. Families' Advice to Agencies

Based on their experiences with adopting, families were asked to provide advice to agency staff. They mentioned most often the need for adequate resources and services for *both* the family and child (n = 59, 37 percent). These included post-adoption services such as subsidies, respite, support groups, and counseling. Forty-eight families (30 percent) indicated that they needed information about the process and the child's background, as well as referrals for services. Other advice included: communicate with families in a timely and honest manner and provide parents with realistic information about the child's potential outcomes based on his/her history (n = 32, 20 percent); provide good training for agency staff members, prospective adoptive families and adoptive families, including useful parenting tools and adequate preparation for both the parents and child for the adoption process (n = 29, 18 percent); be supportive and encouraging to all types of families during the process as well as after finalization (n = 26, 16 percent); display a commitment to the process, including finding the best possible family for a child and placing the child's needs above standard agency practices (n = 20, 12 percent); and avoid displaying bias towards families and advocate for both the family and the child (n = 15, nine percent).

In summary, adoptive parents felt it was most important that families approach adopting a child or children from the foster care system with commitment to the child and to the process and a willingness to remain flexible, tolerant, and patient. Families need to maintain and display unconditional love for the child, as well as a sense of humor. Adoptive parents felt that agencies need to provide services and resources to support the child and the family. They also expressed that agencies should provide adequate information about the adoption process and the child's background, as well as referrals for services.

Table 44. Advice to Prospective Adoptive Families*

Type of Advice	Number	Percent**
Families must be committed to child/adoption process	38	24%
Flexibility, tolerance, patience, unconditional love, and a sense of humor	31	19%
Families need to advocate for child	22	14%
Families must have realistic expectations of child	19	12%
Families need to be open-minded regarding contact	15	9%
Meeting other foster/adoptive parents is important	13	8%
Families should foster the child before adopting him/her	12	7%
Families must be open to resources/services	12	7%

*Percentages are calculated on the total number of families in the sample (N = 161).

**Percentages do not add to 100% because parents may have reported more than one response.

Table 45. Advice to Agencies*

Type of Advice	Number	Percent**
Have resources and services available	59	37%
Provide information and referrals	48	30%
Communicate in a timely/honest manner	32	20%
Offer good training and preparation	29	18%
Support and encourage families	26	16%
Commit to the adoption process	20	12%
Advocate for/be unbiased towards family	15	9%

*Percentages are calculated on the total number of families in the sample (N = 161).
**Percentages do not add to 100% because parents may have reported more than one response.

APPENDIX A: BARRIERS STUDY

Child, Family, and Agency Factors influencing the Adoption Process

All barrier and success codes were grouped thematically into factors. The factors fall into three categories: agency, family, and child factors. Each factor can have a positive or negative valence; for example, the factor "agency emotional support" could occur as a barrier if the family reported that they did not receive the level of emotional support they needed fromtheir agency during the adoption process, or it could occur as a success factor if a family reported that a high level of emotional support from their agency helped them during the adoption process.

Child Factors

Child's attachment

Includes the child's ability to attach to adoptive family members and their level of attachment.

Foster care experiences and history

Includes experiences in foster care, such as length of time in care; the number of placements a child has had; and the quality of care, such as abusive or caring foster parents. Also included is child preparation for the adoption and other history, such as reason for coming into care.

Child's behavior

Includes the presence of child strengths or challenging behaviors. Examples of strengths include being loving and kind, having a good sense of humor, or being perceived as a "great kid." Examples of challenges include running away, chronic lying, hoarding food, animal cruelty, substance abuse, tantrums, aggression, and parentified behavior. [28]

Child's health

Includes the child's health, such as HIV status, special medical needs, and being terminally ill.

Child's mental health

Includes the child's mental and emotional health; for example, psychiatric diagnoses, need for psychotropic medications, and difficulty controlling emotions.

Child's educational needs

Includes the child's educational needs such as learning disabilities, developmental and cognitive delays, and mental retardation.

Child demographics

Includes the child's age and race/ethnicity.

Family Factors

Family commitment

Includes the family's level of commitment to the adoption process, a child who has been referred or placed with them, and the child's adoption into the family.

Family's ability to interact with systems

Includes the family's efforts and success in working with systems for the child and family's benefit. Systems include the child welfare system and the agency, the school system, mental health systems, service providers for additional ADD/ADHD and attachment disorder training and resources.

Support systems

Includes adoptive parents' formal and informal sources of emotional and practical support, including support groups, family, and friends.

Family preparation and expectations

Includes the adoptive parents' level of preparation for adoption, such as training and life experiences that have helped prepare them for adoption and parenting. Also included are their expectations of the child's behavior and achievement.

Parent-child match

Includes the extent to which the parents feel that a child who has been referred or placed is a good match with their family including temperament, interests, appearance, and cultural, racial and ethnic background.

Family composition

Includes family size, marital status, and family composition, such as the presence of biological, foster, or other adopted children being parented at the same time as the adopted child.

Family dynamics

Includes the level of family functioning prior to the child's adoption, such as the physical and mental health of family and the way they relate to each other.

Child integration

Includes the ability of the adoptive family to fully accept and integrate the child as a family member, while simultaneously acknowledging and respecting his/her past attachments and history.

Parenting ability and temperament

Includes the parents' skill in parenting, such as the ability to use effective, non-punitive discipline and important features of temperament such as flexibility, ability to provide structure, stress management, and a sense of humor.

Family distress at placement disruption/Child no longer available

Includes the experience of families who have had the placement of one or more children disrupt, or who sought to adopt a particular child who became unavailable for adoption (e.g. the child returned to the biological family or was adopted by foster parents).

Change in personal circumstances

Includes instances in which a family's level of commitment to the adoption process changed due to personal circumstances such as loss of income, pregnancy, serious illness, or relocation.

Agency Factors

Availability of services

Includes the extent to which the agency provides pre- and post-adoption services to the child and family, such as therapy, respite, and support groups.

Agency emotional support

Includes the extent to which the agency partners with the family in the process of adopting the child—how encouraging, helpful, and emotionally supportive the staff are to the family.

Availability of financial support

Includes financial issues, such as subsidy availability or fees incurred during the application process.

Adoption process logistics

Includes the level of bureaucratic "red tape" that parents experience while trying to adopt the child, how easy and quick the process is, and any errors and inconveniences experienced, such as redundant, delayed, or lost paperwork.

Legal system interactions

Includes experiences related to the legalities of the adoption process, such as the termination of parental rights and the finalization of the adoption. It includes the agency's ability to provide assistance with legalities, legal process and delays, and the family's interactions with others such as the guardian ad litem or judge.

Jurisdictional and inter-jurisdictional issues

Includes the level of difficulty encountered by parents in the adoption process when working with more than one agency or with two different counties, regions, or States. This factor includes issues between public and private agencies and issues with Interstate Compact on the Placement of Children.

Family assessment

This factor includes the agency's effective screening and assessment of parents for their suitability to raising children with special needs.

Level of agency bias and cultural competence

Includes the agency's non-biased and fair treatment of diverse family types and the level of cultural competence of staff members. It includes families' experiences of bias based on race/ethnicity, marital status, sexual orientation, age, financial status, and religion. It includes experiences with others in the system beyond the family agency (e.g. discrimination by child's agency, judge).

Agency communication/responsiveness

Includes agency practices related to communication, such as timely responses and access to complete and accurate information. It includes the level of effective and thorough assistance families received during the process of adopting.

Adoption Exchanges

Includes the adoptive family's experiences with adoption exchanges; whether the exchanges were easy to use and helpful in finding a child to adopt; and whether agency staff were responsive to their inquires.

APPENDIX B : TOP BARRIERS

As part of the Barriers study, this table reports the total number of families in all five groups citing child, family, and agency factors as "top barriers" to their adoption process.

	Discontinued during Orientation/ Application (n = 5)		Discontinued prior to Completion of Training/Home Study (n = 27)		Discontinued after Approval (No Placement) (n = 53)		Discontinued after Disrupted Placement (No Finalization) (n = 17)		Finalized (n = 98)	
Child's attachment	0	0%	0	0%	1	2%	2	12%	3	3%
Foster care experiences and history	0	0%	0	0%	3	6%	3	18%	6	6%
Child's behavior	0	0%	0	0%	1	2%	1	6%	6	6%
Child's health	0	0%	0	0%	1	2%	0	0%	0	0%
Child's mental health	0	0%	0	0%	2	4%	1	6%	1	1%
Child's educational needs	0	0%	0	0%	0	0%	0	0%	1	1%
Child demographics	0	0%	0	0%	1	2%	0	0%	0	0%
Family commitment	2	40%	1	4%	5	9%	2	12%	6	6%
Family's ability to interact with systems	0	0%	0	0%	0	0%	0	0%	1	1%
Support systems	0	0%	0	0%	1	2%	1	6%	0	0%
Family preparation and expectations	1	20%	4	15%	4	8%	1	6%	9	9%
Parent-child match	0	0%	0	0%	4	8%	3	18%	2	2%

(Continued)

	Discontinued during Orientation/Application (n = 5)		Discontinued prior to Completion of Training/Home Study (n = 27)		Discontinued after Approval (No Placement) (n = 53)		Discontinued after Disrupted Placement (No Finalization) (n = 17)		Finalized (n = 98)	
Family composition	0	0%	1	4%	2	4%	0	0%	4	4%
Family dynamics	1	20%	2	7%	4	8%	2	12%	0	0%
Child integration	0	0%	0	0%	1	2%	2	12%	4	4%
Parenting ability and temperament	0	0%	1	4%	1	2%	1	6%	0	0%
Family distress at placement disruption/child no longer available	0	0%	0	0%	1	2%	11	65%	1	1%
Change in personal circumstances	1	20%	9	33%	14	26%	1	6%	1	1%
Availability of services	0	0%	1	4%	6	11%	5	29%	15	15%
Agency emotional support	0	0%	7	26%	22	42%	12	71%	23	23%
Availability of financial support	0	0%	0	0%	0	0%	0	0%	1	1%
Adoption process logistics	1	20%	11	41%	27	51%	7	41%	67	68%
Legal system interactions	0	0%	0	0%	0	0%	3	18%	11	11%
Jurisdictional/ Inter-jurisdictional issues	0	0%	0	0%	7	13%	3	18%	14	14%
Family assessment	0	0%	1	4%	0	0%	1	6%	4	4%
Level of agency bias and cultural competence	0	0%	2	7%	6	11%	3	18%	10	10%
Agency communication/responsiveness	0	0%	9	33%	26	49%	8	47%	45	46%
Adoption exchanges	0	0%	0	0%	2	4%	0	0%	1	1%

OVERALL BARRIERS

	Discontinued during Orientation/Application (n = 5)		Discontinued prior to Completion of Training/Home Study (n = 27)		Discontinued after Approval (No Placement) (n = 53)		Discontinued after Disrupted Placement (No Finalization) (n = 17)		Finalized (n = 98)	
Child's attachment	0	0%	2	7%	3	6%	5	29%	4	4%
Foster care experiences and history	0	0%	1	4%	14	26%	9	53%	25	26%
Child's behavior	0	0%	2	7%	3	6%	2	12%	14	14%
Child's health	0	0%	0	0%	4	8%	1	6%	2	2%
Child's mental health	1	20%	3	11%	6	11%	2	12%	4	4%
Child's educational needs	0	0%	0	0%	0	0%	1	6%	2	2%
Child demographics	0	0%	0	0%	1	2%	0	0%	0	0%
Family commitment	3	60%	5	19%	9	17%	4	24%	18	18%
Family's ability to interact with systems	0	0%	0	0%	1	2%	0	0%	1	1%
Support systems	0	0%	1	4%	3	6%	4	24%	1	1%
Family preparation and expectations	1	20%	5	19%	11	21%	4	24%	15	15%
Parent-child match	1	20%	5	19%	12	23%	7	41%	9	9%
Family composition	2	40%	5	19%	6	11%	0	0%	10	10%
Family dynamics	1	20%	5	19%	9	17%	4%	24%	2	2%
Child integration	0	0%	2	7%	5	9%	2	12%	9	9%
Parenting ability and temperament	0	0%	4	15%	2	4%	3	18%	2	2%
Family distress at placement disruption/child no longer available	1	20%	0	0%	2	4%	16	94%	2	2%

(Continued)

	Discontinued during Orientation/Application (n = 5)		Discontinued prior to Completion of Training/Home Study (n = 27)		Discontinued after Approval (No Placement) (n = 53)		Discontinued after Disrupted Placement (No Finalization) (n = 17)		Finalized (n = 98)	
Change in personal circumstances	1	20%	10	37%	17	32%	1	6%	2	2%
Availability of services	0	0%	4	15%	14	26%	9	53%	38	39%
Agency emotional support	1	20%	16	59%	40	75%	15	88%	58	59%
Availability of financial support	1	20%	2	7%	2	4%	1	6%	13	13%
Adoption process logistics	3	60%	22	81%	50	94%	14	82%	96	98%
Legal system interactions	0	0%	0	0%	4	8%	4	24%	26	27%
Jurisdictional/ Inter-jurisdictional issues	0	0%	3	11%	15	28%	5	29%	29	30%
Family assessment	2	40%	4	15%	2	4%	1	6%	12	12%
Level of agency bias and cultural competence	0	0%	8	30%	15	28%	5	29%	22	22%
Agency communication/responsiveness	1	20%	19	70%	46	87%	15	88%	78	80%
Adoption exchanges	0	0%	0	0%	5	9%	0	0%	11	11%

*Percentages are calculated on the total for each column (e.g., n = 5 families who discontinued during orientation/application).

**Percentages do not add to 100% because multiple barriers could apply to each family.

REFERENCES

Abidin, R. R. (1995). *Parenting Stress Index: Professional manual*. Odessa, FL: Psychological Assessment Resources.

Adoption and Safe Families Act of 1997, Pub. L. No. 105–89.

American Public Human Services Association. (2006). *History of the ICPC*. Washington, D.C.: American Public Human Services Association.

Fowers, B. J. & Olson, D. H. (1993). ENRICH marital satisfaction scale: A brief research and clinical tool. *Journal of Family Psychology, 7*, 176-185.

Reilly, T., & Platz, L. (2003). Characteristics and challenges of families who adopt children with special needs: An empirical study. *Children and Youth Services Review, 25*(10), 78 1-803. Rycus, J. S., Freundlich, M., Hughes, R. C., Keefer, B., & Oakes, E. J. (2006). Confronting barriers to adoption success. *Family Court Review, 44*(2), 210-230.

Smith, S. L. (2005). Safeguarding interstate adoptions: The Interstate Compact on the Placement of Children. Retrieved April 7, 2008, from *http:// www.adoptioninstitute.org/publications/2005_Brief_Safeguarding_Interst ate_* Adoptions%20_April.pdf

U.S. Department of Health and Human Services. (2005). *Adoptions of children with public child welfare agency involvement by State: FY 1995 - FY 2003*. Washington D.C.: Author.

U.S. Department of Health and Human Services. (2006a). Adoption incentive program: Fiscal year 2005 earning year. Retrieved November 17, 2006, from http://www.acf.hhs.gov/news/press/2006/adoption incentive prog.htm

U.S. Department of Health and Human Services. (2006b). Adoption incentives and AFCARSpenalties; Adoption Promotion Act of 2003 (Public Law 108-145): Information memorandum. Retrieved November 18, 2006, from http://www.acf.hhs.gov/programs/cb/laws

U.S. Department of Health and Human Services. (2006c). AFCARS report - Preliminary FY 2005 estimates as of September 2006 (13). Retrieved November 16, 2006, from *http://www.acf.hhs.gov/programs/cb/stats _research/afcars/tar*

U.S. Department of Health and Human Services. (2006d). AFCARS report: Final estimates for FY1998 through FY2002 (12). Retrieved November 16, 2006, from *http://www.acf.hhs.gov/programs/cb/stats_research /afcars/tar*

U.S. Department of Health and Human Services. (2007). AFCARS report: Trends in Foster Care and Adoption, FY2000 through FY 2005. Retrieved

November 19, 2007 from *http://www.acf.hhs.gov/programs/cb/stats_research/afcars/trends.htm*

U.S. General Accounting Office. (2002). *Foster care: Recent legislation helps States focus on finding permanent homes for children, but long-standing barriers remain (GA O-02-585)*. Washington, D.C.: Author.

End Notes

[1] Percentages do not always add up to 100% due to rounding.

[2] Includes the level of difficulty encountered by parents in the adoption process when working with more than one agency or with two different counties, regions or States. This factor includes issues between public and private agencies and issues with the InterState Compact on the Placement of Children.

[3] Findings must be interpreted with caution, as samples in each State are not representative and may not include responses from both public and private agency staff. Of the 29 States and the District of Columbia, there were seven States from which both public and private agency surveys were received. These States include Arizona, California, Colorado, Illinois, Minnesota, Mississippi, and Texas. Of these seven, three are among the States with the highest numbers of available children waiting for adoption: Texas with 10,147 waiting children, California with 4,903 waiting children, and Illinois with 3,621 waiting children.

[4] InterState Compact on the Placement of Children (ICPC) is the statutory law and contract that guides placement of children across State lines. The goal of ICPC is to provide a legal and administrative framework for the placement of children across State lines in order to ensure that children placed in other States receive the same services and legal protections that would be provided to them if they remained in their home State. In addition, the compact specifies legal, financial, and supervisory responsibilities for the State placing the child, as well as the State receiving the child (American Public Human Services Association, 2006). ICPC facilitates all interjurisdictional foster care placements, adoptive placements, and relative placements for children in the child welfare system.

[5] In this analysis, 59 private agency staff and 78 public agency staff located in Arizona, California, Colorado, Illinois, Michigan, Mississippi, and Texas were included.

[6] Although the majority of current adopters of children from foster care are foster parents who have had a prior relationship with the child, agencies are continuing to struggle to conduct targeted and general recruitment for families to adopt the many waiting children whom foster parents are not adopting. Many of these are older children who belong to sibling groups. Therefore, we decided deliberately to over-sample non-foster parent adopters (general adopters) to better understand family dynamics in cases in which the family and child have not had a prior relationship, and therefore learn more about factors that lead to their success.

[7] Eighteen percent of the 28 families had voluntary contact with birthparents pre-finalization that stopped after finalization.

[8] Percentages do not always add to 100% due to rounding.

[9] Is it important to note that families may have provided responses they felt were more socially desirable.

[10] Inter-country adoption refers to adoptions in which the child and the adoptive family are residents of two different countries.

[11] In the group of nine children who had siblings, three children were half siblings who were placed together in one adoptive home; the other six children had siblings who were either

adopted by other families, placed with a relative, had different permanency goals, or whose whereabouts were unknown to the prospective adoptive parents. The 10 children who were indicated as not having siblings may have had siblings that the prospective adoptive parents did not know about or did not report.

[12] See the appendix for barrier factors' definitions and tables showing detailed response information.

[13] The top barriers reported for the five groups of families are the most critical 2-3 barriers reported by families. Most families reported experiencing a total of at least 15 barriers during the adoption process.

[14] For categorical items, comparisons were conducted using Fisher's Exact Test, a non-parametric alternative to the chi-square test of independence used when sample sizes are small and expected frequencies are low.

[15] The Games-Howell was used because it is robust even with unequal group sizes, violations to normality, and unequal variances.

[16] Percentages do not add to 100% because participants could have mentioned more than one family factor.

[17] Findings must be interpreted with caution, as samples in each State are not representative and may not include responses from both public and private agency staff. Of the 29 States and the District of Columbia, there were seven States from which both public and private agency surveys were received. These States include Arizona, California, Colorado, Illinois, Minnesota, Mississippi, and Texas. Of these seven, three are among the States with the highest numbers of available children waiting for adoption: Texas with 10,147 waiting children, California with 4,903 waiting children, and Illinois with 3,621 waiting children.

[18] The Interstate Compact on Adoption and Medical Assistance (ICAMA) of 1986 was enacted to coordinate the provision of adoption subsidies, medical assistance, and post-adoption services to children placed for adoption across State lines (Rycus, Freundlich, Hughes, Keefer, & Oakes, 2006). ICAMA ensures that children placed for adoption across State lines who are eligible for Title IV-E assistance are able to receive medical services. However, ICAMA does not guarantee medical coverage for children who are not Title IV-E eligible. Eligibility for medical coverage for a child who does not qualify for Title IV-E assistance must be negotiated between the sending and receiving State and/or county child welfare systems. Typically, the sending State agrees to pay for the child's medical expenses until the adoption is finalized and the child becomes a legal resident of the receiving State (Smith, 2005).

[19] Legal services might include assistance for families with a child involved in the juvenile justice system.

[20] Emergency shelter care is a temporary, out-of-home placement for a child taken into State custody care. This is typically a short-term placement for a child while decisions are being made about where the child will live.

[21] Pearson's correlation measures the magnitude and direction of a linear association between two variables. Pearson's correlation can range between -1 and +1. The closer the correlation is to either -1 or +1, the stronger the association. A correlation of 0 indicates no association between the two variables. Positive correlations indicate that as one variable increases, so does the other, while negative correlations indicate the opposite, as one variable increases, the other decreases.

[22] For parents with more than one child, this measure applies to all children being parented (including adopted, biological and foster children).

[23] Pearson's correlation measures the magnitude and direction of a linear association between two variables. Pearson's correlation can range between -1 and +1. The closer the correlation is to either -1 or +1, the stronger the association. A correlation of 0 indicates no association between the two variables. Positive correlations indicate that as one variable increases, so does the other, while negative correlations indicate the opposite, as one variable increases, the other decreases.

[24] For categorical items (i.e., race/ethnicity), comparisons were conducted using either the chi-square test of independence or its non-parametric alternative, Fisher's Exact Test (used when sample sizes are small and expected frequencies are low). Continuous variables (i.e., age at placement) were analyzed using independent samples t-tests.

[25] Forty-five adoptive families had contact with birthmothers, and 20 adoptive families had contact with birthfathers. Percentages are based on 45 when calculated for birthmothers and 20 when calculated for birthfathers.

[26] Some parents answered this question with multiple reasons, so the percentages do not add up to 100%.

[27] Eighteen percent of the 28 families had voluntary contact with birthparents pre-finalization that stopped after finalization.

[28] Parentified behavior occurs when a child attempts to assume a parenting role with his/her siblings, thereby causing disruptions to the adoptive family structure. This can happen with biological siblings who are adopted together when one child in the sibling group formerly had "adult-like" responsibility for siblings in the biological home.

In: Barriers and Success Factors in Adoptions... ISBN: 978-1-61209-740-4
Editor: Bradley J. Carson

Chapter 2

THE AFCARS REPORT

United States Department of Health and Human Services

PRELIMINARY FY 2009 ESTIMATES AS OF JULY 2010 (17)

Source: Adoption and Foster Care Analysis and Reporting System (AFCARS) FY 2009 data (October 1, 2008 through September 30, 2009).

Notes: Data from both the regular and revised AFCARS file submissions received by July 29, 2010 are included in the information below. Missing data are excluded from the distributions presented below.

How Many Children were in Foster Care on September 30, 2009? 423,773

What were the ages of the children in foster care?

Mean Age	9.6	
Median Age	9.7	
Less than 1 Year	6%	24,505
1 Year	7%	31,141
2 Years	7%	28,304

(Continued)

3 Years	6%	24,356
4 Years	5%	21,447
5 Years	5%	19,443
6 Years	4%	18,099
7 Years	4%	17,143
8 Years	4%	16,750
9 Years	4%	15,902
10 Years	4%	15,693
11 Years	4%	15,597
12 Years	4%	16,227
13 Years	4%	18,371
14 Years	5%	22,366
15 Years	7%	28,549
16 Years	8%	34,989
17 Years	9%	36,079
18 Years	3%	11,697
19 Years	1%	4,002
20 Years	1%	2,634

What were the lengths of stay of children in foster care?

Mean Months	26.7	
Median Months	15.4	
Less than 1 Month	5%	21,375
1 - 5 Months	19%	82,514
6 - 11 Months	18%	74,731
12 - 17 Months	13%	56,977
18 - 23 Months	9%	38,533
24 - 29 Months	7%	30,164
30 - 35 Months	5%	22,259
3 - 4 Years	12%	49,122
5 Years or More	11%	48,088

What were the placement settings of children in foster care?

Pre-Adoptive Home	4%	17,280
Foster Family Home (Relative)	24%	101,688
Foster Family Home (Non-Relative)	48%	200,179
Group Home	6%	25,302
Institution	10%	40,502
Supervised Independent Living	1%	4,690
Runaway	2%	8,047
Trial Home Visit	5%	23,010

What were the case goals of the children in foster care?

Reunify with Parent(s) or Principal Caretaker(s)	49%	202,065
Live with Other Relative(s)	4%	14,763
Adoption	25%	102,615
Long Term Foster Care	8%	32,361
Emancipation	6%	26,547
Guardianship	4%	15,990
Case Plan Goal Not Yet Established	4%	16,280

What was the gender of the children in foster care?

Male	53%	222,685
Female	47%	200,999

What was the race/ethnicity of the children in foster care?

Alaska Native/American Indian	2%	8,491
Asian	1%	2,603
Black	30%	127,821
Hawaiian/Other Pacific Islander	0%	792
Hispanic (of any race)	20%	86,581
White	40%	167,235
Unknown/Unable to Determine	2%	8,118
Two or more races	5%	21,584

Note: Using U.S. Bureau of the Census standards, all races exclude children of Hispanic origin. Beginning in FY 2000, children could be identified with more than one race designation.

How Many Children Entered Foster Care during FY 2009? 255,418

What were the ages of the children who entered care during FY 2009?

Mean Age	7.9	
Median Age	7.1	
Less than 1 Year	16%	40,931
1 Year	8%	19,230
2 Years	7%	16,701
3 Years	6%	14,021
4 Years	5%	12,717
5 Years	4%	11,372
6 Years	4%	10,755
7 Years	4%	9,951
8 Years	4%	9,230
9 Years	3%	8,711
10 Years	3%	8,234
11 Years	3%	8,232
12 Years	4%	9,069
13 Years	4%	10,984
14 Years	6%	14,279
15 Years	7%	18,074
16 Years	7%	18,611
17 Years	5%	12,436
18 Years	0%	633
19 Years	0%	91
20 Years	0%	43

What was the race/ethnicity of the children who entered care during FY 2009?

Alaska Native/American Indian	2%	5,450
Asian	1%	2,189
Black	25%	64,690
Hawaiian/Other Pacific Islander	0%	630
Hispanic (of any race)	20%	51,628
White	44%	110,933
Unknown/Unable to Determine	3%	6,500
Two or more races	5%	12,566

Note: Using U.S. Bureau of the Census standards, all races exclude children of Hispanic origin. Beginning in FY 2000, children could be identified with more than one race designation.

How Many Children Exited Foster Care during FY 2009? 276,266

What were the ages of the children who exited care during FY 2009?

Mean Age	9.6	
Median Age	8.9	
Less than 1 Year	5%	12,409
1 Year	8%	21,070
2 Years	8%	21,525
3 Years	7%	18,204
4 Years	6%	15,674
5 Years	5%	13,846
6 Years	5%	12,700
7 Years	4%	11,890
8 Years	4%	10,860
9 Years	4%	10,065
10 Years	3%	9,549
11 Years	3%	8,794
12 Years	3%	8,630
13 Years	3%	9,040
14 Years	4%	10,936
15 Years	5%	13,621
16 Years	6%	16,323
17 Years	6%	17,514
18 Years	10%	26,416
19 Years	2%	4,213
20 Years	1%	1,837

What were the outcomes for the children exiting foster care during FY 2009?

Reunification with Parent(s) or Primary Caretaker(s)	51%	140,061
Living with Other Relative(s)	8%	21,424
Adoption	20%	55,684
Emancipation	11%	29,471
Guardianship	7%	19,290
Transfer to Another Agency	2%	6,291
Runaway	1%	2,141
Death of Child	0%	417

Note: Deaths are attributable to a variety of causes including medical conditions, accidents, and homicide.

What were the lengths of stay of the children who exited foster care during FY 2009?

Mean Months	22.0	
Median Months	13.7	
Less than 1 Month	13%	35,340
1 - 5 Months	15%	41,459
6 - 11 Months	18%	49,475
12 - 17 Months	14%	38,631
18 - 23 Months	10%	28,110
24 - 29 Months	7%	20,673
30 - 35 Months	5%	14,932
3 - 4 Years	10%	28,226
5 Years or More	7%	19,307

What was the race/ethnicity of the children who exited care during FY 2009?

Alaska Native/American Indian	2%	5,389
Asian	1%	2,111
Black	27%	74,264
Hawaiian/Other Pacific Islander	0%	674
Hispanic (of any race)	20%	55,200
White	43%	118,422
Unknown/Unable to Determine	2%	6,062
Two or more races	5%	13,573

Note: Using U.S. Bureau of the Census standards, all races exclude children of Hispanic origin. Beginning in FY 2000, children could be identified with more than one race designation.

How Many Children were Waiting to be Adopted on September 30, 2009? 114,556

Notes: Waiting children are identified as children who have a goal of adoption and/or whose parental rights have been terminated. Children 16 years old and older whose parents' parental rights have been terminated and who have a goal of emancipation have been excluded from the estimate.

What is the gender distribution of the waiting children?

Male	53%	60,287
Female	47%	54,269

How many months have the waiting children been in continuous foster care?

Mean Months	38.0	
Median Months	29.0	
Less than 1 Month	1%	661
1 - 5 Months	4%	4,991
6 - 11 Months	8%	9,206
12 - 17 Months	13%	15,313
18 - 23 Months	14%	15,479
24 - 29 Months	12%	14,248
30 - 35 Months	10%	11,015
36 - 59 Months	22%	24,773
60 or more Months	16%	18,876

What is the racial/ethnic distribution of the waiting children?

Alaska Native/American Indian	2%	1,920
Asian	0%	535
Black	30%	34,088
Hawaiian/Other Pacific Islander	0%	213
Hispanic (of any race)	22%	25,231
White	38%	43,918
Unknown/Unable to Determine	2%	1,807
Two or more races	6%	6,807

Note: Using U.S. Bureau of the Census standards, all races exclude children of Hispanic origin. Beginning in FY 2000, children could be identified with more than one race designation.

How old were the waiting children when they were removed from their parents or caretakers?

Mean Age	5.0	
Median Age	4.1	
Less than 1 Year	25%	28,315
1 Year	9%	10,092
2 Years	8%	8,800
3 Years	7%	7,998
4 Years	7%	7,686
5 Years	7%	7,404
6 Years	6%	7,150
7 Years	6%	6,578
8 Years	5%	6,177
9 Years	5%	5,343
10 Years	4%	4,718
11 Years	3%	3,954
12 Years	3%	3,304
13 Years	2%	2,545
14 Years	2%	1,792
15 Years	1%	1,037
16 Years	0%	450
17 Years	0%	89

Where were the waiting children living on September 30, 2009?

Pre-Adoptive Home	14%	15,759
Foster Family Home (Relative)	22%	25,165
Foster Family Home (Non-Relative)	54%	61,362
Group Home	3%	3,980
Institution	6%	6,331
Supervised Independent Living	0%	128
Runaway	1%	636
Trial Home Visit	1%	725

How old were the waiting children on September 30, 2009?

Mean Age	8.1	
Median Age	7.5	
Less than 1 Year	4%	4,351
1 Year	9%	9,817
2 Years	9%	9,953
3 Years	8%	8,767
4 Years	7%	7,800
5 Years	6%	7,054
6 Years	6%	6,515
7 Years	5%	6,225
8 Years	5%	6,023
9 Years	5%	5,884
10 Years	5%	5,635
11 Years	5%	5,534
12 Years	5%	5,373
13 Years	5%	5,335
14 Years	5%	5,547
15 Years	5%	5,814
16 Years	4%	5,014
17 Years	3%	3,921

How Many Children in Foster Care Had their Parental Rights Terminated for All Living Parents? 69,947

As of September 30, 2009, how many months had elapsed since the parental rights of these foster children were terminated?

Mean Months	24.6
Median Months	12.7

How Many Children were Adopted with Public Agency Involvement in FY 2009? 57,466

Source: Adoptions can be reported to the AFCARS adoption database at any time after the adoption has been finalized. This chapter includes adoptions finalized in FY 2009 reported in regular and revised submissions by July 29, 2010.

What is the gender distribution of the children adopted from the public foster care system?

Male	51%	29,146
Female	49%	28,306

How old were the children when they were adopted from the public foster care system?

Mean Age	6.3	
Median Age	5.2	
Less than 1 Year	2%	1,136
1 Year	11%	6,486
2 Years	15%	8,366
3 Years	11%	6,543
4 Years	9%	5,270
5 Years	8%	4,505
6 Years	7%	3,904
7 Years	6%	3,478
8 Years	5%	3,096
9 Years	5%	2,642
10 Years	4%	2,418
11 Years	4%	2,042
12 Years	3%	1,812
13 Years	3%	1,523
14 Years	2%	1,308
15 Years	2%	1,091
16 Years	2%	911
17 Years	1%	725
18 Years	0%	150
19 Years	0%	24
20 Years	0%	14

Notes: The number of adoptions reported here do not equal the number of adoption discharges reported under foster care exits because the adoptions reported here include adoptions of some children who were not in foster care but received other support from the public agency. Missing data are not used in the calculation of the percentages.

What percentage of the children adopted receive an adoption subsidy?

Yes	88%	50,481
No	12%	6,754

What is the racial/ethnic distribution of the children adopted from the public foster care system?

Alaska Native/American Indian	2%	923
Asian	0%	280
Black	25%	14,211
Hawaiian/Other Pacific Islander	0%	120
Hispanic (of any race)	21%	11,878
White	44%	25,418
Unknown/Unable to Determine	2%	874
Two or more races	7%	3,754

Note: Using U.S. Bureau of the Census standards, all races exclude children of Hispanic origin. Beginning in FY 2000, children could be identified with more than one race designation.

How many months did it take after termination of parental rights for the children to be adopted?

Mean Months	13.9	
Median Months	10.2	
Less than 1 Month	2%	1,373
1 - 5 Months	23%	13,007
6 - 11 Months	33%	18,326
12 - 17 Months	18%	10,242
18 - 23 Months	10%	5,364
24 - 29 Months	5%	2,867
30 - 35 Months	3%	1,648
3 - 4 Years	4%	2,299
5 Years or More	2%	867

What is the family structure of the child's adoptive family?

Married Couple	66%	36,133
Unmarried Couple	2%	1,299
Single Female	28%	15,408
Single Male	3%	1,567

What was the relationship of the adoptive parents to the child prior to the adoption?

Non-Relative	14%	7,637
Foster Parent	54%	29,417
Stepparent	0%	120
Other Relative	32%	17,300

In: Barriers and Success Factors in Adoptions… ISBN: 978-1-61209-740-4
Editor: Bradley J. Carson

Chapter 3

TRENDS IN FOSTER CARE AND ADOPTION: (FY2002 - FY2009)

AFCARS Data, United States Children's Bureau, Administration for Children and Families

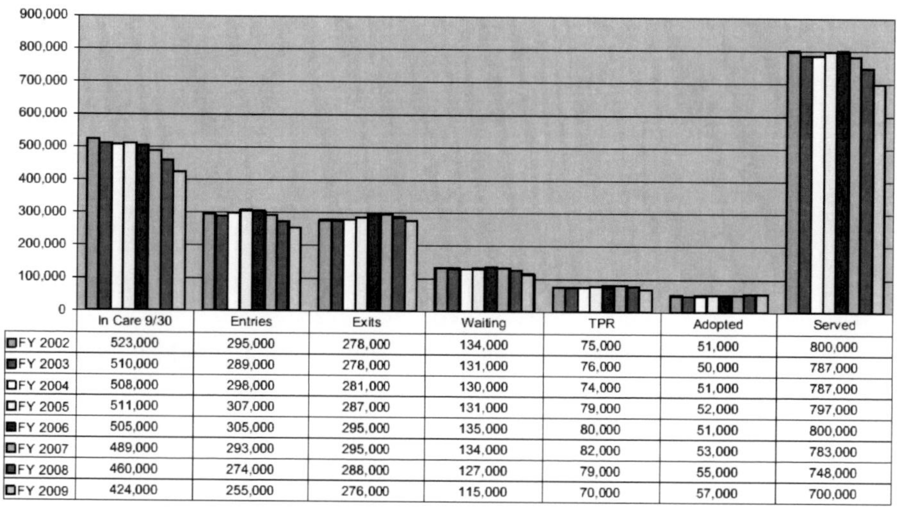

	In Care 9/30	Entries	Exits	Waiting	TPR	Adopted	Served
FY 2002	523,000	295,000	278,000	134,000	75,000	51,000	800,000
FY 2003	510,000	289,000	278,000	131,000	76,000	50,000	787,000
FY 2004	508,000	298,000	281,000	130,000	74,000	51,000	787,000
FY 2005	511,000	307,000	287,000	131,000	79,000	52,000	797,000
FY 2006	505,000	305,000	295,000	135,000	80,000	51,000	800,000
FY 2007	489,000	293,000	295,000	134,000	82,000	53,000	783,000
FY 2008	460,000	274,000	288,000	127,000	79,000	55,000	748,000
FY 2009	424,000	255,000	276,000	115,000	70,000	57,000	700,000

Source: AFCARS data, U.S. Children's Bureau, Administration for Children and Families

Trends in Foster Care and Adoption—FY 2002-FY 2009 (Based on data submitted by States as of July 29, 2010)

DISCUSSION OF TRENDS CHART

This chart includes data submitted to the Adoption and Foster Care Analysis and Reporting System (AFCARS) by States, the District of Columbia and Puerto Rico by July 29, 2010. Please note that, for all of the years shown, some of the data may differ from that shown in earlier versions of this chart. This is due to the fact that some States have resubmitted their AFCARS data after addressing data quality issues.

FFY = Federal Fiscal Year (October 1 through September 30)

Sub-population Definitions

1. **In Care 9/30:** This is an estimated count of all the children in foster care **on the last day** of the FFY. An individual child is included in the count for each year for which he or she is in foster care on the last day.
2. **Entries**: This is an estimated count of all children who entered foster care **during** the FFY. An individual child is counted only once for each year, even if the child entered, exited and reentered care during the year. The most recent date of removal from home is used to determine whether the child entered foster care during the period. If an individual child entered in one year and then exits and re-enters in a subsequent year, he or she is included in the count of entries for both years.
3. **Exits:** This is an estimated count of all children who exited foster care during the FFY **at the end of their most recent foster care episode**. An individual child is counted only once for each year, even if the child exited, re-entered and exited again during the year. The most recent date of discharge (from foster care) is the one counted. If an individual child exited care in one year and then re-enters and exits again in a subsequent year, he or she is included in the count of exits for both years.
4. **TPR (Termination of Parental Rights):** This is an estimated count of all children in care **on the last day** of the FFY whose parental rights have been terminated and who are waiting for adoption. An

individual child who has these characteristics on the last day of the year is counted only once for that year.

5. **Waiting:** This is an estimated count of all children who are waiting to be adopted **on the last day** of the FFY. An individual child is included in the count for each year in which he or she is waiting to be adopted on the last day. There is no Federal definition for children waiting to be adopted. For the purposes of this analysis, children waiting to be adopted include children with a goal of adoption and/or whose parental rights have been terminated. The "waiting" population excludes children whose parents' rights have been terminated, who are 16 years old and older, and who have a goal of emancipation. An individual child is included in the count for each year that he or she has these characteristics on the last day of the year.
6. **Adopted:** This is an estimated count of all children adopted with public child welfare agency involvement **during the FFY.** An individual child is counted only once for each year, even if (in rare cases) the child was adopted multiple times during the year. In cases when an individual child is adopted in one year and then adopted again in a subsequent year, he or she is included in the count of adoptions for both years.
7. **Served:** This is an estimated count of all children who were in the public foster care system **during the FFY.** This number is the sum of two mutually exclusive groups of children: the children who are already in care on the first day of the fiscal year (as of October 1) and the children who enter foster care during the year. An individual child is counted only once for each year.

Technical Discussion

Even though the number of children served is calculated by summing the children in care on the first day of the year plus the entries into foster during the year, another way of counting the number of children served is by adding the number of children in foster care on the last day of the year to the number of exits from foster care during the FFY. We compared the numbers derived from both approaches, and they are equal in FFY 2006, FFY 2008 and FFY 2009, but there is less than a one percent discrepancy in the other years. Most of these differences can be attributed to rounding.

Because the number of entries exceeds the number of exits from FFY 2002 to FFY 2006, we would expect that the number of children\youth in care as of September 30th would have increased during this period. This, however, did not occur, as the number of children in care actually declined. The primary contributing factor to this phenomenon is that, in the AFCARS database, each child is counted only once and the information included on the child in the database is from their most recent foster care episode. However, there are some children who were in foster care on the first day of the year but exited and re-entered during the year one or more times prior to entering their most recent foster care episode. In addition, they remained in foster care through the last day of the fiscal year (September 30) in their most recent foster care episode. In these circumstances, the exit associated with their "in care" status on the first day of the year is not counted, even though it occurred during the fiscal year. We estimate the number of these uncounted exits to be approximately 6,000 per year.

There is also a data quality issue that has had an impact on the number of exits. AFCARS data are submitted every six months and cover a six-month period. Sometimes a child who is reported during one six-month period does not appear in the next period, and there is no record that the child exited. Reviews of these cases have shown that the majority are situations in which the child actually exited, but the exit was not reported to AFCARS. However, because the actual number of these "dropped" exits cannot be calculated, they have not been accounted for in the exit count. As this issue has been brought to the attention of States, the quality of the data has improved dramatically and the number of dropped cases has decreased. For instance, the number of these dropped cases has declined from around 8,000 in FY 2006 to about 3,000 in FY 2007 and FY2008, and about 4,000 in FY 2009. Therefore, these dropped cases constitute less than 2 percent of the reported discharges in the three most recent years.

Data Discussion

Children in Foster Care on September 30th: The data show a decline in the number of children in foster care on the last day of each federal fiscal year (September 30) between FY 2002 and FY 2009, with a small exception in FY2005. A similar pattern is seen in the total number of children served during these years. The number of children served has declined by 100,000 children between FY 2002 and FY 2009 (from 800,000 to 700,000).

Entries into and Exits from Foster Care: In FY 2005, the number of entries into foster care reached its highest point to date with 307,000 entries reported that year. Since that time, however, the number of entries has declined to 255,000 in FY 2009, the lowest number since AFCARS data have been reported. The number of exits, which increased between FY 2002 (278,000) and FY 2007 (295,000), declined to 276,000 in FY 2009, excluding children who exited but re-entered during the same year and children whose discharge dates were missing from the file (see technical discussion above). Beginning in FY 2007 and continuing through FY 2009, the number of exits is greater than the number of entries into foster care.

Children Waiting to be Adopted: Since FY 2006, the number of children waiting to be adopted has been declining (from 135,000 in FY 2006 to 115,000 in FY 2009). The number of waiting children whose parental rights had been terminated as of the last day of the year increased from 74,000 in FY 2004 to 82,000 in FY 2007. The number then declined in FY 2008 to 79,000 and was down to 70,000 in FY 2009. However, as a percentage of the children waiting to be adopted, those children whose parental rights had been terminated has stayed relatively stable, constituting between 61 and 62 percent of the waiting children in FY 2007, FY 2008 and FY 2009, representing an increase over the earlier years (56% in FY 2002) .

Children Adopted: Between FY 2002 and FY 2006, the number of adoptions remained relatively flat, ranging between 50,000 and 52,000. Beginning with the FY 2007 data, we see an increase from 53,000 in FY 2007 to 55,000 in FY 2008 to 57,000 in FY 2009.

CHAPTER SOURCES

The following chapters have been previously published:

Chapter 1 – This is an edited, excerpted and augmented edition of a United Department of Human Services Administration for Children and Families Report to Congress, dated 2007.

Chapter 2 – This is an edited, excerpted and augmented edition of a United Department of Human Services Administration for Children and Families Preliminary Report, dated July 2010.

Chapter 3 – This is an edited, excerpted and augmented edition of a United Department of Human Services Administration for Children and Families Trends in Foster Care and Adoption data, dated July 29, 2010.

INDEX

A

B

C

D

E

F

G

H

I

U

V

W